D0233028

AUTOBIOGRAPHY

OF A

Wardrobe

AUTOBIOGRAPHY

OF A

WARDROBE

by the Wardrobe of Elizabeth Kendall

Illustrations by Laurie Pincus

PANTHEON BOOKS   NEW YORK

LIBRARY OF CONGRESS CATALOGING-IN-PUBLICATION DATA

KENDALL, ELIZABETH, [DATE]
AUTOBIOGRAPHY OF A WARDROBE / ELIZABETH KENDALL.
P. CM.
ISBN 978-0-375-42500-4
1. KENDALL, ELIZABETH, 1947-   2. AUTHORS, AMERICAN—20TH CENTURY—
BIOGRAPHY.   I. TITLE.
PS3611.E5337Z46 2008
813'.6—DC22   2007033613

WWW.PANTHEONBOOKS.COM

BOOK DESIGN BY IRIS WEINSTEIN
PRINTED IN THE UNITED STATES OF AMERICA
FIRST EDITION

2 4 6 8 9 7 5 3 1

The remaining dresses, though they had lost their fresh-ness, still kept the long unerring lines, the sweep and ampli-tude of the great artist's stroke, and as she spread them out on the bed the scenes in which they had been worn rose vividly before her. An association lurked in every fold; each fall of lace and gleam of embroidery was like a letter in the record of her past.

EDITH WHARTON, *The House of Mirth*

Do people have time to feel pain when they are shot? What on earth will Alyosha and Vasya say when they have to fill in forms about their parents? What a shame about that new silk dress that fitted me so well and that I never had a chance to wear. . . .

EUGENIA GINZBURG, *Journey into the Whirlwind*

Will the frock I wept in
Answer me to wear?

EMILY DICKINSON, "Before the ice is in the pools—"

AUTOBIOGRAPHY

OF A

Wardrobe

B. sat on the floor in a dark classroom with the other grad students. It was Sensitivity Training. The teacher told them to close their eyes and imagine in their hands, a book. The book was their own autobiography and they should start to read it.

B. gripped the book tightly, took a breath, opened her eyes, and began to read—about something she had no idea she remembered. It was herself, when small, climbing out of the lower bunk in the early morning, crossing the room to a white dresser, opening a bottom drawer to find a pile of small red corduroy overalls that smelled clean. She took one off the top of the pile.

There was I, present in her deepest of memories. I am B.'s wardrobe, her ever-evolving second skin. She is My inhabitant, My partner, My Body—My B.

From way back in time, those overalls were telling the grown B. who she had been; who she still was. They were hers alone. *I* was hers alone—and have remained so, through upheaval, sturm und drang. I am her language, of body and style. I am soundless and mute, but extremely expressive.

What B. must remember (what she sometimes forgets) is how much wisdom and common sense is stored in Me, from My ancient past.

If bodies and wardrobes can keep such things in mind, can listen to each other—I don't mean fuse together, but not abandon each other either—what can result is a habit of communication that has surprise in it. Such communication does not breed inertia, but the opposite. It's like a marriage that's alive. Or like a friendship that grows over years, until the friends have gotten to an instantaneous understanding of each other's thoughts.

B. and I—after much pain and sorrow—we are finally friends.

This is My story of that friendship.

F ive-year-old B. in a daffodil-yellow pinafore and a white blouse with puffed sleeves stands at the end of a chintz couch, in the midst of grandparents, aunts, and parents. The pinafore has embroidery on the skirt and a wide yellow sash tied at the back of the waist. B. is leaning into the mother, who is sitting on the couch holding a baby brother. On B.'s feet are red "party shoes" with ankle straps and white socks. At her right temple, a white barrette holds back straight, fine dishwater-blond hair.

This dress can stand as well as any for My birth. Wardrobes start out like children, without conscious identity. I was the emanation of the family at the Country Club on a spring day, in a large midwestern city, just after midcentury. Technically, I suppose I'd been born earlier, in a downtown cathedral, as a long, white, lace-trimmed christening gown (overly long, because that's how the Middle Ages phrased its wish for babies to live and grow). Or else in the preverbal moment when the very small B. took out the red corduroy overalls.

But that day at the Club was when I first knew Myself, when I suddenly heard what B. was saying to Me: "You smell clean. You are the color of lemon pie. You have a story on your skirt."

Adults had bent down to read the embroidery on the skirt, then patted B.'s head. What they'd seen were red-thread birds and brown-thread squiggles among green-thread sprinkles, and underneath, the sewn red words "The early bird gets the worm."

Only Americans had put words on clothes—then. At that moment (it was the 1950s), words on clothes were a new idea. In this case they were a message from the business community that had bought the dress.

The rest of Me that day matched the style of the little girls' clothes in books read to B. at home: *Peter Pan, The Little Princess,* the ubiquitous *Alice's Adventures in Wonderland.* B. was sashed, buttoned, and hairbrushed into an immaculate Edwardian wrapping, missing only Alice's horizontally striped stockings.

How did I, a wardrobe, know I was antique at birth? That's what I do. I pick up intimations of sartorial history.

Other family members in that tableau were not

thinking "history," but merely checking off *the right thing* on each other: cinch belts on the young aunts; tweed suits on the older ladies; red bow ties on the older men; spectator pumps on the young mother. And for a small female like B., it was de rigueur to wear a crisp sashed cotton dress and these exact red shoes with a thin strap around the ankle and a red grosgrain bow (like a bow tie) on the toe. This dress code had come from the young mother. Astonished, like so many postwar brides, at having been promoted from ingenue to matron, she couldn't yet imagine a new era. She dressed B. as if she were not her child, but a version of herself as a child, before the war.

So: I came into being in the last moments of that two-centuries-old institution called Childhood, in which everything was *ironed*: collars, sashes, sailor suits. Nowadays it's different. The other day B. saw a mother and small daughter in a New York café. (This is how we communicate: B. sees something and I breathe it in, and catalogue it.) The little girl was wearing a small wrinkled jeans cargo skirt and a miniature cardigan sweater; her *mother* had on a large cotton pinafore.

When I was born, old persons' garments and young persons' garments belonged to very separate spheres.

In My childhood I was more like the 1835 wardrobe of young Toni Buddenbrooks than like today's American child wardrobes. On the first page of that wonderful capitalist saga by Thomas Mann, eight-year-old Toni, "in a dress of shimmering silk," reads aloud to her extended family, the catechism about the Lord having made man and all he owns. And everyone laughs at a *little girl* spouting the capitalist creed.

It was the same a hundred-odd years later at the country club. B., through Me, reflected back what the family wanted to see.

But she herself was not convinced. What she did most of that day was stare at the words on her skirt and think, "Does the early bird really get the worm? What if another bird came later? Maybe another worm would be emerging and the late bird would get *that* worm."

B. looked properly docile on the outside; on the inside she was full of questions. And her first questions were about Me.

Behind the yellow-pinafored B., the mother, seated on the couch, holding the little brother, wears a light blue shirtwaist dress with a full skirt, a thin white belt, and navy-and-white spectator pumps. And behind the couch the father paces, wearing white shirtsleeves and a blue plaid bow tie, holding an amber-colored drink in his hand.

The wardrobes of the mother and father were My immediate ancestors. The problem was: they were such young wardrobes (because of the war) that they didn't know themselves. Back home on a living room side table stood a head shot in a silver frame: the black-haired father as a full-dress marine. Uniforms had delayed his coming of age and his wardrobe's. Uniforms had crowded out all the other clothes until the end of the war, when he was twenty-four. But by then he was married and a father.

Now, at any rate, his wardrobe was in search of a self. For the Country Club lunch the father had put on the same dark gray suit as the family elders, but he'd taken off the jacket—that was daring. And his bow tie was not red like the elders' bow ties but made of faded blue plaid Madras (cotton cloth transplanted from southern India to the golf course). The blue Madras tie was attempting insouciance. Also if you got close to the father's white shirt you could see the slightly rough weave of Egyptian cotton. He liked the feel of that cotton and bought the finest shirts even on a young family's tight budget. At ankle level, his black socks were smooth: garters under his pants kept them up.

War had retarded the mother's wardrobe, too, but her clothes weren't even looking for a coherent self. The spectator pumps on her feet said "haute couture"; her dress said *Oklahoma!* She didn't see the contradiction. Besides, even holding her toddler-son and resting a hand on daughter-B.'s shoulder, she looked too young to be a mother.

She was not exactly invested in her relations with her wardrobe. She was so full of ideals, so thrilled by the new United Nations and the prospect of raising bright little tolerant children that she failed to pay it much attention.

The father was almost a dandy. The mother was not. She always looked slim and neat but liked shortcuts, such as dispensing with "rollers" to curl her hair. Instead she just flipped the ends up by tying a scarf around her head at night. Goodness mattered to her, not clothes. Clothes mattered to the father, not goodness.

B. was close to the mother and wary of the father. But I got more of My deep-down core identity from that father's wardrobe. I was imbued early on with the feel of those Egyptian cotton shirts and the pungent scent of Bay Rum that wafted from the bathroom in the mornings.

Maybe that's why I was interested, from the beginning, in the borderline where male and female clothes met but didn't fraternize—at least not in My early years (they would later).

Here's what My admiration of the father's wardrobe gave the young Me: a taste for rebellion. Or at least a strong impulse to resist the demure, the nice, the "girly."

But you mustn't think Me an orphan without female elders. I had a splendid mentor: the wardrobe of the paternal grandmother.

In this Country Club tableau of My birth, this tall grandmother dominates, sitting in an armchair beside the chintz couch containing B. and mother and brother. A tweed suit jacket hangs like a cape on her shoulders. A double strand of pearls circles her neck, which rises to a long wrinkled face with marceled gray hair. Large pearl drops grace her ears. Removed and returned to her mouth in the flow of talk is a black cigarette holder containing a Benson and Hedges. Long legs with too-thin calves, encased in seamed stockings, end in fine-shaped walking shoes.

The paternal grandfather reclines in an adjacent armchair: bristle-mustached, a soft green-heather tweed jacket sheathing his portly form. Wardrobe-wise, he almost holds his own next to her.

Side by side on a couch opposite sit the *other* grandparents, the maternal ones, who, though richer, pale beside the paternal. He, small, Buddha-bald, drained of color in a beige three-piece suit; she, dark-haired, with slanting-down dark eyes, in a drooping knockoff of a Chanel suit.

At the end of the lunch the tall paternal grandmother leads the way out, heels clicking on the red tiled floor. She is helped into a long, pale beige, double-breasted polo coat with three close-together pairs of big, round mother-of-pearl buttons down the front.

This grandmother liked coats. People do, I think, who have itinerant childhoods. She had had a father trying to shake TB at a string of sanatoriums, trailed by his young family. Her polo coat from that faraway Country Club day is now hanging in the back of B.'s closet, a part of Me. B. wears it sometimes, but doesn't quite have the height to pull it off. Two other coats of the paternal grandmother hang there, too: a nut-brown fur cape (squirrel) that drips off B.'s back, and a long caramel brown suede coat with a red plaid lining and a tab collar.

This latter coat, My favorite, was made by Bonnie

Cashin. It serves as proof that this grandmother loved her wardrobe enough to notice what Cashin and her twin American genius, Claire McCardell (*I* call them twins), were doing in the 1950s: devising the clean, modernist, unfussy shape for women to go with America's rise to mastery on the world stage. Remember that the world-mastery shape didn't swagger in those days. The Cashin-McCardell clothes were simple, sinuous, and meant for motion. Cashin's (and the grandmother's and B.'s) caramel brown suede coat hangs straight down, its plain façade broken only by five small brass buttons down its front and two breast-level pockets adorned with a button each. Such a shape serves above all to give the wearer room to stride out.

The paternal grandmother's clothes showed Me early on that the aim of a wardrobe should be to move freely, in concert with a body. As in a conversation.

4 DOLLS

Books about dolls gave the young B. her first great expectations about Me.

Sara Crewe, heroine of *A Little Princess* (1905), has a large intelligent-looking doll, Emily, with a lavish wardrobe, handmade at a real children's, not a doll's, outfitter. Sara is the very rich little girl left by her father in a London boarding school who becomes the school's scullery maid when the father dies penniless in India, then its princess again when the father's partner finds her by chance, in the garret, and showers her with presents (the sumptuous Emily sitting impassively throughout, in the corner, in a "frock" of lace or velvet or muslin).

Flora McFlimsey, in *Miss Flora McFlimsey's Christmas Eve* (1949), is a doll herself—blond, quaint, forgotten in the attic with her trunk of elaborate old-fashioned clothes. Polished up along with her clothes, she triumphs on Christmas morning as a gift to a youngest daughter, in a family where older daughters dominate.

These two stories were read to B. at the time the father had just quit banking to be a commodity broker. Some days he came home rich and some days poor. The household was tense. A second little brother had arrived and another baby was on the way. Abandoned little girls in books made for good reading, especially if they had dolls or *were* dolls, *with wardrobes*. Into B.'s young mind came the shadowy thought that a wardrobe might be enough of a companion to compensate for human neglect.

That's how *I* started to be, in B.'s mind, not just a bunch of clothes but a friend. A friend with many faces, who could respond, as no one else, to moods, needs, desires, and dreams.

A real doll appeared to underscore this thought— Cissy, from Madame Alexander. Cissy was discovered among many Cissies on a high shelf in Spicer's Toy Store. She had lustrous black saran hair and forward-reaching tan vinyl arms, and wore a blue-and-green taffeta dress with white pantaloons showing under-neath. But additional outfits could be bought for Cissy, complete with little purses and shoes. The additional outfits came singly in powder-blue boxes crisscrossed with flowers and Madame's repeated signature, and on top, cellophane windows framing them.

Unfortunately none of these additional outfits could be bought right then since the family had come up against "a hard time with your dad's job." "Cissy really needs more clothes," said B. "And she needs a friend. She's my only older doll. The rest are babies."

Christmas approached. Parental signals indicated a second Cissy in the offing.

But on the Christmas morning when the new Cissy should have sat among B.'s presents, a strange doll appeared instead. She had dark brown, lusterless hair, not gleaming like Cissy's. Her arms were hard, yellowish plastic instead of plump, pink vinyl. She had a shiny hard-plastic face with a child's full cheeks, and smallish eyes instead of the adolescent wide eyes of the new dolls like Cissy. And the "skin" of her face had little spidery cracks in it.

And yet—this strange new doll came with a trunk of her own, light blue, which opened into two parts, each lined with faded rose-sprigged fabric and each containing a row of miniature doll–size clothes on miniature hangers. Among the clothes were a doll-size light blue wool coat with black piping on the wide collar, a matching light blue beret with a black rim, a doll-size cotton lawn yellow-print summer dress with lace trim on puffed sleeves.

The clothes, a little faded like the doll, were anyway fascinating because they sported tucks and gathers, lace trim on sleeves, contrast-color piping on waists and hems, little pearl buttons on dresses, and small, doll-size sashes in back.

B. didn't know what to say to the mother, who was hovering nearby. The doll was named Sallie, the mother said. And the hair . . . "She has real human hair," added the mother, as B. fingered the hair. "It's my own hair," she explained. "Sallie was my doll, but she went to the hospital and got cleaned up, and she got new hair—from me."

B., kneeling on the floor, playing with Sallie, set her face in a mask of delight.

But sometimes a look of real wonder flitted across B.'s set face, since I was there, whispering to her a surprising thought: that old doll clothes were more delicate, more intricate, more precious than any outfit Cissy would wear.

5 SWIMMING

The aquatic part of My nature in the early 1950s pro-
gressed as follows: dark blue little boy's bathing
briefs, then a silver square tin can, then a little girl's reddish bathing suit with a placket for the nonexistent bust.

The boy's briefs were put on B. at three years old,
just before she was thrown into the Country Club
pool's shallow end, to flounder toward the swim coach,
who was walking backward in the rippling sunny
water. She managed to reach his outstretched arms
and not drown.

The tin can she received after that. Strapped on her
back by means of a clothesline looped around her
chest, it kept her afloat. It glinted in the sun. B. was
proud of it, since cans were awarded only to three-
year-olds who'd survived the throwing in. For Me it
was good too: My first "peer signifying" item.

Most important on the list, the little-girl suit with

the front placket, which arrived after B. had learned not only to swim but to jump into the pool holding her nose. The suit was reddish knit with miniature white seahorses on it. Its underside was the reverse, more white than red.

The suit meant that I accompanied B. in daily splashing moments during the acquisition of the breaststroke and the crawl, and also for the ceremonial first dive. One evening when the other screaming children had left, Coach led B. in the reddish suit down to the dark turquoise deep end of the pool and unfolded a white towel on the edge. B. knelt on the towel and put her hands together above her head. Coach put his own tanned arm in front of her and said, "Go over it." She and I paused, then went over upside-down, into the other, turquoise element.

The reddish suit, a Jantzen, made by the company that had invented stretch swimsuits in 1913, came to symbolize for B. her then free-squirming tadpole body, about which she has often thought with bewildered nostalgia. She thought of it first when she made the swim team and the team received black suits in the new fabric of nylon, suits that were supposed to make bodies go faster in the water. Early nylon swimsuits had an extra piece of nylon, like a web, between the legs. Speedo, the nylon suit company, must have worried about its clinging properties when wet. B. found the between-the-legs web interesting and grown-up but was dismayed at how, higher up, the thin black nylon, when wet, put her stomach in relief, in contrast to the first reddish Jantzen, to which memory had attached no stomach.

B. thought of the reddish suit for years, every time she got a new bathing suit that promised to make her sleek but never did. A dark blue tropical-leafy Hawaiian-print cotton suit with boy legs that ballooned in the water. A yellow-and-black Speedo that wouldn't stay down on the butt; a leopard-skin one-piece that left red marks on the shoulders; a bikini of blue and pink stripes that squeezed at the hips. All were failures for Me, except a lightweight fake-denim maillot that B. bought impulsively years later in a sleazy shop on the Greek island of Santorini. That suit so streamlined her (or so she thought) as she dove into a turquoise pool on a blinding white terrace that she almost reached a mystical accord in memory with the reddish suit.

Still, she kept for many years a fading snapshot of her small self in the reddish suit and a white bathing cap, standing with the little brother against a sunny brick wall by the pool; both skinny, with bony knees; both squinting at the camera.

The little brother stayed as he was in the snapshot for a long time; B. began to grow, right after it was taken. (But she kept the bony knees.)

The tale of Cinderella made its appearance. B. saw a rendition of it in a school auditorium—her first play—enacted by some young wives of the Junior League. A friend of the mother's played Cinderella (somebody B. knew!). Onstage this ragged Cinderella was surprised by a kindly older lady in silver, who waved a silvery wand. The younger actress went off-stage for a moment and came back wearing a glittery lavender dress, which would have been labeled bad taste if it hadn't been magic.

The idea that loneliness and rags were synonymous entered B.'s head. And the mother gave her the record of the *Cinderella* music by Prokofiev. It played over and over on B.'s small white record player, conjuring visions of a palace façade in the moonlight, a cobblestoned avenue snaking into the distance, a curlicued silver coach melting to pumpkin-size . . .

B. pleaded with the mother to make a *Cinderella* play happen for her. The mother gathered some mothers and daughters from B.'s Sunday School class. A *Cinderella* was rehearsed and performed for a small audience of parents, but the mother thought it would be show-offy for B. to play the lead in a play she herself was hosting. B. got the wicked stepmother role instead. As a costume, she got a low-cut green gown with water stains, found in the maternal grandparents' attic. It was too big, but the mother stuffed it with pillows, and put circles of red lipstick on B.'s cheeks.

In My opinion, B. shouldn't have had to play somebody fat. However, her green stepmother gown turned out to be more interesting to Me, more subtle in texture and cut (it was made of stiff grosgrain), than the shiny striped satin gown that Cinderella wore.

Anyway, I embraced at that moment the concept (not yet the reality) of magic clothes, transformative clothes, made of fairy materials like thistle and moonlight, clothes that seemed to mark a body for some higher fate.

Cinderella is the ur-text for wardrobes.

The concept of transformative clothes was reinforced by regular doses of fairy tales administered to B.

by the mother. A dusty bookshelf upstairs in the maternal grandparents' dark Tudor house held old fairy-tale books with faded covers and titles in fancy script, sometimes stamped in gold. The best one was *Told Under the Green Umbrella*.

A t the beginning of the second grade a vision of a saddle shoe came into B.'s head. It was the first vision connected with Me. The urgency of it overcame every obstacle to its being realized (not enough money; you already have shoes for school; a different kind of people from us wear saddle shoes; et cetera).

The shoes glowed even after they'd been bought and had morphed from visionary to real objects in B.'s closet. They smelled like new rubber; the black "saddle" lay over the blazingly white shoe; a rubber sole the color of a human tongue protruded from the shoe's body. From above one saw a black-and-white continent rimmed by pink.

B. thought the saddle shoe vision had sprung immaculate from the place in her brain that created desires. Actually it was a symbol, of the new continent of school, of the smell of sharpened pencils, of starting life over as a person whom one's family didn't know, in the society of other young bodies with *their* new wardrobes.

And of something else I'm sorry to have to write about. Memory connects the shoes with B.'s thickening torso, over which were pulled school dresses and sundresses. The thickening torso had followed the removal of B.'s tonsils, in the hospital, abandoned by the mother for the night, or that's how it seemed (though once when the little brother had been in the hospital, the mother had stayed the night with him; but he'd been only two). Ice cream was prescribed in the hospital for lacerated throats. Eating the ice cream had made B. big, or that's how she explained the phenomenon to herself.

As for Me, I had the tricky task of adapting to B.'s new size, and those saddle shoes helped. They were not small and red like little girls' shoes, but big, and black and white. B. assumed a stony expression when she put them on, which meant: "So what if I'm not small like the other siblings?" It also meant, when directed at the mother alone: "I know what's going on in the world of style and you don't."

This was true in a way. The mother had put B. in public school because of her civic ideals, even though she herself had gone to private school, as had all her friends, as did all of her friends' children, B.'s wary and supercilious playmates at the Country Club.

So B. had to figure out, alone, with only Me to help—and I was still so young—what were the aesthetics of the public school she'd been thrown into. Our "taste" became flashier than the mother's, as indicated by those shoes. Saddle shoes, despite their high-flown origins as pseudo golf shoes on the feet of the Prince of Wales during a 1930s visit to America, belonged, in the fifties, not to royalty but to a mass-market world: the child breeding grounds that were the new suburbs.

What the saddle shoes really marked for B. was the beginning of a struggle that would take over her life, to become someone who wasn't the mother. And for Me, the struggle to become a wardrobe that wasn't the mother's.

But sometimes B. needed to retreat to a reassuring world unskewed by the contretemps of taste, and I helped her do that, too. She and the mother possessed matching Lanz dresses of dark blue cotton printed with black curlicues. The dresses had high necks, tight waists, full skirts. Necks, waists, and hems were trimmed at the edges with white braid rickrack.

One afternoon those dresses were worn for a mother-daughter piano concert at the maternal grandmother's house, offered to the Wednesday Club. They shone deep blue against the shiny ebony of the two pianos placed curve to curve at the end of the living room. Twenty lady elders watched from green arm-chairs. On opposite ebony piano benches, the mother and B. in those dresses sat, looking like little and big versions of the same thing, except for different hair:

the mother had a dark brown bob and glasses; B. had light brown braids tied at the ends with white ribbons.

In some small part of herself, B. didn't enjoy being almost a copy of the mother, but in another part of herself she wanted to do the mother proud. Benign attention from the Wednesday Club was guaranteed in any case by Lanz of Salzburg, which functioned as the postwar sign of "well-bred," and which brought to the white ladies of the Club a scent of the wholesome Alpine Tyrol, apparently needed in our humid southern midwestern city.

The Wednesday Club did not suspect that small middle-class African American girls downtown were wearing Lanz dresses too, though a few years later the mother would discover the miraculous parallel existence in our city of a world that mirrored her own except it was African American. And much later, in New York, B. would acquire a best friend who was black, from the Midwest, whose own best Lanz dress had been a bright rose pink, with orange lining, and one big ruffle around the collar line.

And Me? On the faraway occasion of B. and the mother playing for the Wednesday Club, I, a spirit, was much freer than she to think outside the sociological box. What *I* got from B.'s Lanz dress was a glimpse of another dead empire, gayer than the one I'd trafficked with up till then.

Salzburg! Hapsburgs! A small bewigged Mozart at a spinet piano, wearing miniature satin breeches and waistcoat (to match his father), with some white lace showing at wrists and neck. Maybe the white rickrack adorning neck and wrists of the 1950s Lanz dresses referred to the well-bred linen that had peeked out from clothes in Hapsburg times.

As for the blue-black Lanz fabric: it was more abstract in its references. Those black curlicues seemed related to the music itself. As B. cast her simple chords into the swirl of melody coming from the mother's piano, those curlicues seemed to dance in their blue surround.

Music always cheers a wardrobe.

9 BALLET

The mother made B. a ballet skirt. It was reversible—turquoise on one side, white with red and green tumbling elves on the other. This garment encapsulated the misery of ballet for B. and therefore for Me, her would-be second skin.

Ballet hadn't been misery at its beginning. Before the first ballet lessons, B. had seen another vision: arched pink toe shoes stabbing the ground.

Then the lessons started. B. and the other five ballet students in her grade at school were driven downtown to the ballet school. But on the way they were ushered into one of their houses and fed gooey donuts for energy—not a good idea before a ballet class. Next to a Peck and Peck's and down some stairs was the ballet school's yellow office, where a perfumy lady sat at a desk. Behind her a window onto a big light studio showed older girls leaping.

B. and the friends were not allowed to leap, yet. Their time in the studio consisted of holding onto a smooth wooden barre, bending their knees to go down and straightening them to go up. And pointing first one foot, then the other. Then they went out onto a sanded wooden floor and did it all over again without a barre. Madame, in pink tunic, named the steps in a melancholy English accent. B. couldn't quite hear and kept getting it wrong.

She got it wrong because of the distraction in the dressing room of her own stomach jiggling as she donned leotard and tights. This was why the mother had made the skirt, to cover up B.'s stomach. She'd made it reversible because, newly economical, she liked the idea of two garments for the price of one. But the doubled fabric of the skirt added to the stomach instead of hiding it.

Despite these doleful sensations or because of them, B. longed even more for the toe shoes. But students had to earn toe shoes in a ritual try-on. Every girl got a try-on, so Madame couldn't deny B. hers, in a gypsy-like inner chamber hung with scarves. "Tie up the ribbons, like so," said Madame. "Now stand up. Now take a step to show me you're properly pulled up." B. could stand in the toe shoes, but beyond that she couldn't move, not even one foot in front of the other, not even in the fifth try-on, when Madame wearily said yes.

The toe shoes were bought. They were mother-of-pearl pink. They were worn once and then abandoned, along with the lessons.

This was a bad moment in the conversation between B. and Me. I couldn't reach her, even through the tights and leotard. Grief and muted rage about her new shape had shut B. off from Me.

10 THE STOMACH

Here I must write about the stomach, a hateful subject. But it's true: as B. grew she didn't just grow taller, she grew bigger, in the middle. And I, scrambling to compensate, to flatter, to respond to her conflicting signals, grew confused and anxious. I couldn't enjoy anything with her at that stage.

Too much anxiety poured, like bile, into the river of our communications.

Why was this?

Really, this subject is beyond My narrative reach. I'm just a wardrobe. But I *can* say that as B. grew, the father turned oddly disdainful. He mentioned B.'s rear end a lot and sometimes addressed her as "Big Butt."

Nowadays B. thinks it was because he was the son of that tall grandmother with all the coats, with the heels that clicked on the floor when she strode. Humorous and cynical about most things, the father always called this grandmother "Mother," with a reverential clench to the facial muscles. Maybe "Mother" had been a bit too much for a small boy to handle. Maybe she'd molded him long ago into a little lackey ready to do her bidding, and now he took it out on weaker females.

Whatever the reason, the sight of B.'s female flesh disrupting the lines of her clothes did not please him.

Meanwhile the mother didn't know what to do with the bigger B. *She* had never "passed through an awkward phase." Old 1930s black-and-white photos in nubby black albums showed the bathing-suited mother as a girl, standing on beaches, always thin, tanned, and serious. Now, when talking to B. about food, she would put on that bright reasonable tone.

"A banana is a good thing if you're still hungry."

B. reached for the cookies.

Back when I started this book I wasn't supposed to mention a certain shorts suit of 1958, but I told B., for the sake of narrative honesty, I must. The family now consisted of five children. Stringent economy meant no shopping in stores. Twice a year, in April and February, the mother shepherded all the siblings to a downtown hotel suite rented by Best & Co., where each kid picked two outfits for the coming season. The outfits straggled through the mail in brown boxes.

There was one shorts suit for which B. checked the mail every day.

It was blue-and-white-checked Bermuda shorts and a sleeveless white seersucker shirt edged with blue-and-white piping. It arrived just before school let out, and B. wore it from the time she took shoes off for summer to the time she put shoes back on to return to school. But it didn't ever give B. the summer heedlessness it was supposed to. On the contrary: this mention of that shorts suit brings a recollection of the bulge in B.'s middle, which was disproportionate to her spindly bare legs. (B. had inherited the paternal grandmother's thin calves.)

Next door to B. lived Toni, a smaller, younger, curly-headed girl. Two houses up from Toni was Kate, a taciturn girl older than B. These two and B. did everything together, including swimming each day in Toni's pool. Yet two of the three always "ganged up" on the other one, and which two it was who were ganging up shifted from day to day.

The shock of one day has remained. Pear-shaped B. in the blue-checked shorts suit arrived at the pool carrying suit and towel, to see two heads already bobbing in the water.

"Who invited you?" they shouted.

B. wasn't ever the Tweedledum she felt herself to be, though family albums show that she was hefty. (Now whenever B. sees a fat girl-child on the street or in the bus, she imagines a grinding fury inside the child. But it's not true of every fat child. Some are more wisely loved than others.)

I want to stop this piece here. I don't like dwelling on that shorts suit. I want to go back to the Hope that it's My job to keep alive.

After ballet B. switched sports. Riding a horse didn't require undressing in a dressing room with other girls. She could put on dungarees at home. Plus: in the dim hay-and-manure-smelling vault of the stable, the older girls currying horses spoke to the younger girls, not like in ballet.

Even Tina with her own horse spoke to B. One day Tina, riding her own horse, invited B., riding the stable horse named Tail-light, because he was so slow his tail was always visible, on a daring expedition out of the stable grounds (normally forbidden), across creeks and woods and backyards to a mansion with many Tudor peaks, where a servant in the kitchen poured orange juice.

Tail-light had woken to a gallop; B. had stayed on.

Tina said B. should try a gymkhana, which was a horse show. But clothing was needed for a gymkhana: jodhpurs, high black boots, tweed jacket, white stock, hunt cap. It cost a lot.

The mother borrowed the jodhpurs and boots from friends with daughters. The tweed jacket and the stock came unexpectedly from a trunk of her own things in the maternal grandparents' attic. She even knew how to twist the stock around B.'s neck and secure it with a gold diaper pin. The black velvet hunt cap had to be bought, for such a large sum I have remembered it: forty dollars.

In front of the mirror in the jodhpurs, jacket, and stock, B. raised her chin and lowered her eyelids. Then she put the black velvet cap over her braids. She stood for a while in the company of her reflection. The shame of the chubbiness melted away.

And Me, I got charged up on the ruthlessness wafting from the costume. Those belled-at-the-thigh jodhpurs, and also the high boots, had been usurped, first by the British army and then by every cavalry corps in old Europe, from Brahmin Indian native dress. The white stock referred back not just to the emergency bandaging of horses but to a line of clothes-conscious Anglo-French dandies from Beau Brummel to Napoleon and the Duke of Wellington, who'd worn such stocks.

All this history encasing the chubby body of an eleven-year-old girl in the American Midwest.

At the first gymkhana, B., in her riding costume, walked for a while around the gymkhana grounds flicking a whip against her leg, greeting even young riders she didn't know and their loud, jodhpured mothers. Then she had to get up on the horse. She patted its neck very hard and pleaded to it sotto voce for help. In the ring she panicked and forgot about spotting which horse shoulder was moving first, so she could adjust her horse-signals to that. Nonetheless she took third in a field of five; she got a yellow roseate ribbon with tails. At another gymkhana she took a fourth. Then she stopped riding.

In school B. was a good student. She knew the answers. She was a reader. She looked acceptable, too, in her crisp cotton dresses, made palatable by the saddle shoes. She played on the swings a lot with girls in her class. She even liked softball because of the running and shouting and being on a team.

It was outside school, in the bodily disciplines that well-bred girls were supposed to practice, among kids she didn't know but who knew each other, that she faltered, and couldn't get her flesh to work with her brain.

That's why I had such trouble helping her. Normally

I enhance the connection between flesh and brain. But I went awry in those years and got My interventions wrong. I didn't conceal B. enough in ballet. In riding I concealed her so much that she stopped believing in My honesty.

Waiting for the twelve-year-old B. in the Best & Co. hotel suite was a new kind of dress: sleeveless red coral with a dropped waist and white piping. And a matching white wool cardigan edged with red piping. A dress with its own sweater! Color-coded, like a two-tone car. The Mouseketeers, pictured in *Mouseketeer Magazine* in their own kitchens or backyards, had such dresses.

The only problem: the mother recoiled from the red coral dress. "It's brassy," she said. "It's not," said B. "It's . . . modern. And if I don't get it, I can't be myself." The mother didn't understand such a sentiment, since she had never felt any passion for her own clothes.

The dress was bought because B. had been given a clothes allowance, which meant she had the power of choice. That was her point in the argument.

The dress arrived in the mail. B. put it on and saw in

the mirror that the bright coral made her yellowish and the dropped waist made her thicker. And where had I been all this time? Excited. Impressed. Teenaged! And then—caught out and crestfallen. I'd been too young to resist the lure of the newfangled.

The mistake of the dress was compounded by another mistake. The mother proposed a symbolic end to childhood. She braided B.'s hair for the last time and cut off both braids, still with light blue grosgrain ribbons on the ends. (The braids with ribbons remain somewhere in B.'s apartment, in a paper bag.) A hair-cutter completed the operation. What was left looked like a thatch. B. couldn't stop crying. A color photo from Easter 1959, taken in the church parking lot—those jewel-toned fifties colors—shows a lot of dressed-up little children and, towering over them, B. as a thickish red-and-white tube, thatched on top.

This was the saddest time of our joint childhoods. Ballet, shorts suit, riding, then this dress. B. and I had lost our intimacy. Getting it back would take a while.

Two party dresses were bought for B.: a tight-waisted black velvet "jumper" that went over a white satin puffed-sleeve blouse; a tight-waisted dove blue velvet dress with short cap sleeves. They were necessary for the invitation-only "fortnightlies," whose existence B. hadn't suspected until the invitation came—even if she'd spent lots of evenings watching the young aunts in the maternal grandparents' house getting dressed for *their* parties.

This should have been B.'s great leap: girl to young lady. But it was too sudden. I was too unsettled to help. Those dresses had been sprung on B. so fast she hadn't had time to have a vision of them. That is, *I* hadn't had time to make a place for them in My idea of Myself.

And another thing: all the fussiness pointed to some

horrible anxiety in the offing. Before the dances, the mother rolled B.'s now longer hair in socks and made pin curls in the front with bobby pins, the whole brushed out just before departure. Then she pinned the bra straps to the dress so they wouldn't show, then straightened the girdle (it took some strength), then rolled up the half-crinoline at the waist so it wouldn't hang below the hem.

The biggest mark against these dresses was, in My opinion, this rubbery armor needed under them, which brought discomfort and shame in its wake. B. already had a "training bra," a minuscule piece of cotton. The new bra she got for those dances was a big white science-fiction thing with points. In the lingerie shops the garrulous old saleslady showed her, by miming, "how to put yourself into it." The girdle was a sheath of rubber pulled on over stomach and rear end, with four stocking tabs (sometimes called suspenders) dangling from it, into each of which was gathered a piece of stocking so as to hold the stockings up, since bare legs couldn't be seen in public. Over the girdle went a stiff half-crinoline.

The history of female undergarments contains a lot of hard moments and a few soft ones. One soft moment came after the French Revolution, when female flesh was let out of girdle prison. Young ladies and old ones in those post-revolutionary years wore nightgown-like dresses of near-transparent muslin or batiste or lawn, which invited contemplation of the supposedly pure Republican flesh underneath. The idea was something like Grecian robes.

Another soft moment came in the early twentieth century, when dancer Isadora Duncan took to wearing Grecian tunics without corsets underneath, in the street, and couturier-showman Paul Poiret inaugurated mock-Oriental velvet tube dresses with much gentler corsets.

Hard Baroque moments had seen young women in stiffened cloth or whalebone stays or horsehair stuffing or rubber—like crustaceans. The moment when B. was coming of age was the hardest of hard moments, though only at pelvis and bust, not at the previously corseted ribs. So, therefore, unstable. On the way to the dances, B.'s inner armor always spiraled out of whack under the dress: the bra twisted one way; the girdle and stockings another. Even spiraled wrong, the girdle gave her the sensation of being punched in the stomach.

Also: the gilded youths at the dances were not B.'s friends from school but instead the old uneasy stranger-playmates of the Country Club, which meant she had no one to talk to among the girls. And the boys were clumped in a corner kicking each other until volunteer mothers grabbed some by the hand and joined them to girls.

B. took her turn in a clumsy foxtrot among other clumsy foxtrotters. This was not how it was supposed to be. In *War and Peace* (another empire panorama), which B. was avidly reading, the boys had worn white uniforms to balls: elkskin pants under regimental jackets featuring gold braid at the shoulders, gold buttons down the fronts, nipped-in waists, silk stockings, and buckled dancing slippers. Not shapeless dark suits and big black shoes, like the boys at B.'s fortnightly.

In *War and Peace,* Natasha Rostova was deliriously happy in a slim white tulle dress over a pink silk slip, with a rose in the bodice (it was that post–French Revolution soft time). She was in harmony with her wardrobe.

At B.'s first ball she was at odds with Me. And no wonder. I was compelled by social anxiety to restrain her in that punched-in-the-stomach posture. Hair curled, hands white-gloved, lips pink-tinted, B. walked around perpetually short of breath, and out of place.

Summer camp sent an exact list of what should go in the trunk, so power of choice was removed. I stood by as B. got ready to go sylvan, in forest green shorts, white shirts, mint green square-tied "ties" that were supposed to hang around the collar with the knot at breast level.

Each camp tent on the side of a mountain contained only one little wavery mirror tacked to a supporting pole, which showed only a wavery reflection. As a result, the crowd of girls forgot about mirrors. Fat girls, thin, tall, short, lanky, roly-poly, lumpy, or sinewy girls—each just put on whatever wrinkled pair of shorts and wrinkled white shirt was nearest, so as to tear up and down the cleared mountainside between lake and woods. Even B. forgot that clothes were meant to hide what the father called her potbelly.

B. was happy. But I was not. I had been so close to

her; I'd been next to her skin and in her thoughts a lot of the time, even in her angry thoughts. Now at camp, what with rushing all over and talking about Goodness, she forgot about Me.

The camp favored the part of a girl that was considerate of others and entertained higher thoughts about God and Nature. No mention was made of second skins. Much mention was made of that other, anachronistic companion to the body—the soul—around a big stone hearth in the old lakeside hall. Even girls with prominent teeth, girls with prissy ways of talking, girls with potbellies, had something to say about that neglected part of them, their souls.

It was only on rainy days, when the costume trunks came out of the attic smelling musty, and disgorging lace, velvet, feathers, and uniforms with gold braid, that awareness of Me returned. Girls trooped to the bathroom shack in back of the kitchen to look in the longer mirror there; they crowded each other out of the way posing in the costumes.

On the last night of camp, a hundred girls sang in a big circle in the main hall, hands on each other's shoulders, firelight on their faces, those ridiculous paramilitary ties around their necks. They sang about the beloved camp and their selfless love for each other that had banished vanity.

Dream on, little girls.

Another vision came to B. immediately after summer camp: a medium-gray Shetland cardigan sporting a grosgrain ribbon down the button line, and a darker, charcoal-colored, pleated wool skirt. B. had never seen such an outfit as far as she knew. It had just popped immaculately into her mind the way the saddle shoes had popped years before. And just as the saddle shoes had been urgently needed for the second grade, the Shetland sweater and skirt were urgently needed for the ninth grade, in B.'s new school, a private school for girls, tuition paid by the maternal grandparents.

But the state of the family finances meant that the Shetland vision could be alluded to by B. only once in a while, in an offhand manner. "Did you see the sweater on that girl over there?" "Isn't gray a comforting color?"

One day, though, after a few weeks, B. came home from school to find the items of the vision draped on her bed, like a schoolgirl flopped on her back. The mother had finally understood how much I meant to B. The mother had become My confederate! That's why she'd made the vision come true, though she'd gotten some details wrong. There was no grosgrain ribbon on the sweater; the skirt was a lighter shade than charcoal.

B. in her guilty gratitude overlooked the flaws.

The gray sweater and the only slightly darker skirt allowed B. to run the gauntlet of cold-eyed fellow fourteen-year-olds at the start of each day. This was My kind of protection: a costume with the power to hide a new girl in plain sight.

But the costume wasn't finished. "The other girls aren't wearing saddle shoes anymore, they're wearing Abercrombies *with flaps,*" said B. to the mother one day after school. Abercrombie and Fitch, hunting and fishing retailers, outfitters of Teddy Roosevelt, had long ago constructed a country lace-up oxford with an ornamental slitted leather "tongue" hiding the shoelaces. Now those Abercrombies had been adopted suddenly, en masse, because the richest girl in B.'s class had "problem feet" and needed to wear them.

After a half-year at the new school, the Abercrombies, smelling of crisp new leather, could be managed. Then B. emerged definitively from the shadow of anxiety to melt into the majority at the school who exuded a precise and peculiar Anglophilia from every item of their wardrobes. Everyone exuded this but a few weird girls who still wore penny loafers or oxfords without flaps.

Once again B. was decked out in, and I defined by, the antique trappings of the British Empire, trappings with (as usual where it concerned the British Empire) a masculine caste. The skirt had box pleats like the Scots warrior kilt; the ribbed knee socks, color-coded to the skirts, also came from Scotland; the Shetland sweater derived from North Sea islands; the lace-up shoes had once served to show off the foot shape of eighteenth-century gentlemen undergraduates.

What was odd was that such an outfit was thought to have seductive powers for girls. Seductive powers were necessary since the boys at the brother school were always visible, though far away, on *their* green playing fields, separated from the girls' green playing fields by a valley and a creek.

But back then, young female eros was hidden under, or else signaled by, boy elements in clothes. Boy elements also indicated the opposite impulse: the mass suburban urge to be respectable. The respectability urge was connected no doubt with the postwar worship of Winston Churchill, with the halcyon economy, the splintering of the American dream into little ranch houses, and the demonization of the Soviets, who were not Anglophiles.

Nabokov (a kind of Anglophile, certainly anti-Soviet) got it right in his eerily smart novel of 1955. Humbert Humbert's first paroxysm came from Lolita's wearing a tartan kilt and a boy's shirt.

B .'s adult figure arrived suddenly in 1963, featuring full hips and small breasts. The reverse would have been helpful. Her old clothes didn't fit her. Her new filled-out shape made Me, or what I had been, obsolete.

B. was sent downtown with two signed blank checks of the mother's to find an Easter dress. An older school friend, Susan, went along. Susan was a beatnik who wore only black or purple. Nevertheless she believed that "the only place to shop" was the cement-colored art-deco downtown Saks Fifth Avenue, inside of which she picked out a plain beige dress and handed it to B.

I did not expect to like a plain beige dress until B. put it on.

It was made of sand-colored raw silk with a sticky woven look. It had short sleeves, a little collar, and a zipper up the front, covered by a placket of dress material. Its shape was A-line: it *indicated* the curves of the female body as if by a hand gently sketching not curves but a supple, geometric triangle with a dip for the waist, which made B.'s new womanly flesh almost okay.

It was very light on the hanger.

It cost fifty dollars, a sum that made B.'s heart beat from terror.

"You need pumps," said Susan, and found B. soft, black, high-cut leather pumps trimmed at the rims with beige curlicues and signed inside by a lady designer named Margaret Jerrold. They also cost fifty dollars. B., spellbound by the person looking back from the mirror who had jumped over adolescence, filled in the sum on each check. Upon seeing the purchases, the mother turned deathly pale. "I have never spent that much money on a dress," she said, "much less shoes."

The mother was occupied at that time with the care of B.'s second little sister, born mentally retarded. When she went out with the father to cocktail parties she still looked slim and bright, but at home she had a mother-costume: old wraparound corduroy skirt, cast-off flannel shirt from one of the brothers, loafers with thin white socks, so thin that B. (of the Abercrombies and knee socks) could not help but scorn them.

Looking back I can say that B.'s raw-silk dress was distantly related to the clothes of Jacqueline Kennedy. *Her* achievement as First Lady (and her designer Oleg Cassini's) was a cool, clean, light rendition of womanliness, a womanliness as neutral as a man's business suit.

The dress connects in My memory with a minor operation in the upstairs bathroom, executed on B.'s ears by another new girlfriend. A block of ice, a cork, a needle, the mother hovering outside in the hall—presto, holes in the ears! When B. wore the beige raw-silk dress she also put tiny round gold posts in her ears.

The dress and the gold posts lifted B. on the ladder of sophistication to a rung higher than the mother's. She teetered up there on her high rung looking down at the mother, a vantage point that did not feel good.

For Me the dress marks a historical moment on the edge of a great divide between the era of Definite Olds and Youngs and the wild next era. In hindsight, the dress pulsates with what was to come. It was not meant for a sixteen-year-old. But there was nothing—nothing—in between bland schoolgirl clothes and haughty matron clothes.

No one in our ritual-bound midwestern city had an inkling of how big would be the change that was coming. Not even I had any inkling. But I knew something was not right.

I loved that raw-silk dress and those discreet gold earrings as *objects*. But in My heart of hearts I didn't want to be a detached, polite, and smugly aesthetic wardrobe.

17 ROUGH CLOTHES

The first jolt of the New, for Me and B., came when the father rented a turquoise-and-white mobile home to take him and his favorite red-tailed hawk to a falconry convention in Centerville, South Dakota, the hometown of one of the key practitioners of the ancient sport. In midlife the father had fallen in love with falconry and was trying to make the two younger brothers do the same. He brought them along as entourage.

He brought B. because she had just learned to drive and he couldn't drive all that way himself.

In Centerville, B. trailed half-asleep over muddy fields behind a gaggle of rough-clad men and two pint-size brothers. She wore wool Bermuda shorts, knee socks, and the Abercrombies, which got progressively muddier. Everyone looked up at the birds; B. looked down at her shoes. The Centerville guy's pure white gyrfalcon was named Lena Horne, a beautiful-ugly fact B. couldn't take in, since I was making her so unhappy she couldn't think.

My discomfort drove B. to beg some money from the father, who, surrounded by joking companions with birds on their fists, pulled out some bills. A sporting goods store on Centerville's one-block Main Street disgorged a thick red-and-black plaid wool shirt, olive-drab hunting pants, and lace-up tan boots.

The now burly B. waltzed out into the muddy furrows of spring fields to watch again the falcons swooping on pigeons. They made beautiful loops in the air before pulverizing the pigeons. Afterward B. swaggered around Main St. with the guys and ordered hamburgers like them.

In 1830s Paris the young George Sand had made herself a student's costume of redingote (a long tailored jacket), pants, vest, hat, and cravat, in which she could walk freely around the city. It was the costume of a dandy. The dandy was the first historical personage connected utterly and willfully to clothes, almost created by clothes. Of course the dandy was usually a man. But when Sand disguised herself in the dandy suit, it seemed to her that she could do anything, even "go around the world," because "my clothes feared nothing."

That's how B. felt. Pants on women were new then, having made their appearance only a decade or so before this moment in Centerville. Here I'm not counting thirties movie stars in satin lounging pyjamas and forties Rosie the Riveters in overalls—quickly put aside after the war. Nor am I counting rough pants. In the fifties no rough pants had yet joined wardrobes, only coy ones like Bermudas, capris, pedal pushers, and "dungarees" with gingham cuffs carefully matched to gingham shirts. Even St. Laurent's pantsuits were a few years away.

With these rough pants and killer boots I was transgressing. I was entering what was for Me a new territory of unrestrained locomotion. Which meant I was on my way to abolishing all traces of the smug obedience that belonged to wardrobes then, especially female wardrobes.

eatles' records hit the department stores. *A Hard Day's Night* came to the movie theater. *Life* magazine, weekly companion of lazy moments, began showing skinny shrunken men's suits turning cartwheels over backlit grass and shrunken schoolgirl dresses cavorting in Piccadilly Circus.

But I didn't get the message and neither did My fellow wardrobes of the Midwest. What was the matter with us? Decades of definite Olds and Youngs had slowed Us down (though once I glimpsed the future, when the Royal Ballet was in town and B., in a restaurant with a young man, saw Nureyev enter in a floor-length white leather coat, trailing dancers in fantasy garb).

B. took leave of high school in a stiff white gown, holding one of the ribbons emanating from a Maypole.

Nor did anything change much at Ivy League Radcliffe College, where B. started life over. There, wardrobes contiguous to Me contained ball gowns and skirt suits meant for some invisible highlife and *for the Harvard Library.* Yes, girls went to that old majestic library in high heels, stockings, jewelry, makeup, and skirt suits with girdles underneath, and little purses (and ungainly book bags). No Abercrombies and knee socks in sight. Me, I was panicked: where were these things and how could B. buy them?

B.'s roommate's mother had the answer. B. was flown to Scarsdale for the weekend and driven to some chaotic little streets in downtown Manhattan, with store windows blaring Markdowns! The roommate and her sad-eyed mother found in the markdown bins two wrinkled, twisted discards of navy-and-white-checked wool, which turned out to comprise a little suit: skinny jacket and A-line skirt. The suit, after the cleaner's, smoothed B. in the right places, and its checks were gay and surprising.

Had B. forgotten the fearless moments in the rough clothes? Yes, but so had I in My anxiety. The memory of the rough pants had been left behind in that faraway old world of Home. Now B. had landed in an edgy new world, where life seemed to be a play, but she didn't know her lines and didn't have a costume—not until the blue-checked suit came on the scene.

When it did, B. and the roommate could walk

together into the high-ceilinged old library looking almost like twins, in skirt suits, with their hair brushed to turn *under.* They could sit at a reading table crossing and recrossing their stockinged legs to beguile the poets and section leaders roaming the reference shelves on the sides of the room. They could read Homer in intermittent gulps.

But not for long, since the girdles made them squirm. As did hunger. They were then eating only lettuce and cottage cheese, so as to turn into the rarified creatures sought by poets and section leaders.

And We two wardrobes—I and the roommate's—collaborated in this charade, unaware of being already old-fashioned.

B. made another trip to New York, this time alone, without the roommate. All of a sudden she had someone of her own to visit there, someone who'd given her birthday presents, sent her letters, taken her skiing once. Her middle aunt.

The mother's three younger sisters, a brunette, a blonde, a medium-blonde—the Three Graces of B.'s childhood—had worn their hair in long pageboys. When B. was young they'd still lived at the maternal grandparents' house. A deep closet on the landing of that house had held their long satin ball gowns hung in plastic, their white kid gloves stacked on shelves, their dancing shoes tucked into hanging chintz pockets.

By the time B. went off to college, the first and third aunts had fulfilled the promise of their wardrobes and married nice young men in suits. The middle aunt, the blonde, had not. She'd gone off to Florence, Italy, to study painting. While there, she'd learned some languages and had even written an indignant letter back to the local paper about the Soviet Union invading defenseless Hungary. Then she'd taken a job in New York, where she too had married, but not a businessman. She'd married a tall older opera baritone with a fierce face (he played Herod in Christmas operas). Then she'd gone home to have a baby, and now she was back in the city.

B. was a little afraid of the opera singer uncle, but went down one Thanksgiving anyway to stay for a night with him, the aunt, and the baby in their Upper West Side apartment. B. slept behind a black-and-red Chinese screen in the living room. The aunt, thin, pretty, nervous, smoked a lot and wore creamy heathery colors that seemed to refer to paintings of Florentine madonnas in hazy landscapes. She took B. and the baby on a walk, then to lunch at a café, then to the Met Museum to stare at more Italian paintings. The uncle came home to dinner and told tales of singers on the stage of the Met Opera.

Just before B. left for the evening bus back to college, the aunt called her into the bedroom. "You must come back soon—I'm a little lonely," she said. Then she reached into her closet and brought out the shoes, which "might fit you."

They were Italian shoes of soft brown suede; they had low heels and discreet leather flaps right above the toes. They welcomed B.'s feet gently and firmly. All the way home on the bus B. stared at the Italian shoes on her feet, illuminated by the bus's floor light. They had a flap, like her once-beloved Abercrombies, but the flap was small, just a sketch of a flap, suede-soft not leather-shiny—and the Italian shape was streamlined. The Italian shoes were the Abercrombies grown up, alchemized by the city.

The shoes for Me summed up all the city sights and smells B. had just taken into her senses: the Chinese screen in the aunt's living room, the old black and white tiles in her bathroom, the autumn smell of New York. Back in Cambridge, they definitely enhanced the suavity of the blue-checked skirt suit. I had never encountered Italian shoes before.

What fine things existed in the world, especially in Italy.

The other miracle was that these Italian shoes had come not from Manhattan stores blaring markdowns but from someone in B.'s own family. Someone who had flown out beyond the Midwest into the World, as B. herself longed to do, whatever the cost.

B. had a wistful dream she never told about. Only I knew about it. She dreamed of becoming a Guest Editor for the *Mademoiselle* College Issue.

The College Issue, which came out every August, featured twenty college girls who'd won the Guest Editor contest. They were brought to New York in June, to run around and go to plays, parties, interviews, and to guest-edit the College Issue. Then they traveled all together to a trendy foreign place, where they were photographed, all wearing the same outfits, like twenty twins. The photograph, in a double-page spread, was the pièce de résistance of the College Issue.

I was dubious about those travel outfits, which were very cheerful—one year it was pleated checked skirts and white beanies in Madrid; the next, tweed coats and newsboy caps in Copenhagen; the next, black-and-white travel capes in Mexico.

But B. waited at home for the August issue with beating heart, then pored over it for days, learned the names of the girls, took it with her to college. At college she hid *Mademoiselle,* since Harvard clearly looked down on such lightweight material. Still, something about the traveling and the matching outfits made her restless and wistful.

She even started to work on the contest essay, which was supposed to analyze *Mademoiselle.* But there was this other problem: Guest Editors not only wrote essays, they also modeled clothes, not just in the photos of their trip but in other photos too. And even though it was the pre-Twiggy days and the G.E.'s weren't yet alarmingly thin, B. knew deep down that she herself had a questionable pear shape, despite the cottage cheese diet and the smoothing blue-checked skirt suit.

Most of the time she pretended she didn't. In such pretending, though, there was always, up ahead, a potential jolt, like the invisible step down encountered in dreams.

A tall blond boyfriend of a classmate of B.'s, who rode a motorcycle down from Dartmouth even in winter, told the classmate to tell B. she had "significant thighs."

What did that mean? Was it horrible or complimentary?

B. never figured it out exactly. But the shock had hit her. For three weeks after the boyfriend's pronouncement, she wore even to the library a large concealing sweater that went halfway down her skirts. She had trouble speaking with Me.

And she never entered the *Mademoiselle* contest.

want to write here about the last item to be absorbed into Me before the clothing revolution. It shouldn't be overlooked in the furor, just because it was plain. Besides, it helped Me stay close to the volatile B. through a lot of anguish.

It was a navy blue A-line drip-dry skirt. It was bought for a summer in Europe, where a chambermaid job in a small German hotel awaited B. after her first college year. At the time the Drip-Dry/DuPont on the tag sounded new and chemical. Really the skirt was just an anonymous trapezoid of dark blue that reached to B.'s knees, but it was "practical," which is why the mother sent money for it, the clothes allowance having gone for the plane ticket.

B. wore the plain dark blue skirt under a frilly white apron to clean out rustic German hotel rooms. Wearing the skirt, she shook out the strange duvets, peered at guests' clothes in their closets, leaned out the window to see the little lake below (a lake in German was a *see*), where ducks were swimming, and swept continually so Frau Wegen wouldn't find a crumb on the floor.

The skirt figured in the most poignant moment of that summer: B. leaning on her broom in an empty guest room, telling herself she wasn't lonely because she was her own companion.

She wasn't thinking of Me at that moment, but I, as the skirt, contributed to the bleak comfort she had devised for herself.

Washed and wrung out countless times in the basin, the skirt always dried wrinkle-free. When clothes are washed and dried the smell of their getting wet and then dry ingrains them ever deeper into Me. Even with slightly pungent-smelling DuPont in the fabric. And B. is always happy when clothes come back from drowning.

That skirt drowned and came back to life numbers of times that summer, as B. wore it to visit neighboring towns on days off with Hanseatic cathedrals of red brick; to sit for coffee and cake outdoors with some nice guests from Hanover by another *see*; to perch evenings in the hotel bar. But the skirt got gradually tighter, since on most days after work B. took a book and a bag of cookies to the village cemetery and ate all the cookies while reading. The skirt was nonetheless present in a moment of outrage, one morning at six in the hotel kitchen, when B. found for breakfast only a tureen of goose fat to spread on bread. White goose fat. She suddenly hated the indifferent Frau Wegen and her Germany and all of modern Europe, which she was supposed to be studying when she went home.

The plainness of the skirt, worn every day that summer, must have seeped into My identity and out to B.'s again, because, back home, she switched her object of study from Europe to America. She'd heard in a lecture that the American aesthetic was "form follows function." The words sounded wise. That was the skirt: a wearable trapezoid.

Returned to the right proportions (B. starved off the cookie weight), the dark blue skirt went to classes, paired with a ribbed "poorboy" maroon sweater. It switched back to service-mode evenings, when B. tied on an apron to waitress at the Faculty Club, silently handing plates of food to solitary professors.

That skirt even went, after waitressing, to Student Mixers in the huge old pseudo-Gothic Memorial Hall, and—emboldened by a black turtleneck and high heels—danced.

ere is the moment I've been waiting to write about, the dividing line, the shock that changed My whole being. It didn't come from predictable Mod England but from a distant, wild, and improbable country: Finland.

In Cambridge, Mass., a quaint street near Harvard was lined with white, yellow, and gray Colonial houses turned into shops. They beckoned by means of brick steps leading up to old doors with brass knockers. B.'s "set" of four inseparable friends, living in the same hall, took bicycle detours up and down this street on the way to and from classes. The others, Ronnie, Jamie, Ellen—well heeled through accidents of birth or parental shrewdness—would go into a shop and buy a wood carving, an Eskimo sculpture, a mysterious bold dress.

B. would ride on. With no budget except what 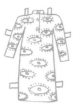 the mother could snag from household expenses, she thought she should resist the little shops, but finally one day she went into the biggest. It occupied three white houses with black shutters. It was called Design Research, DR.

Inside were no confining walls but a huge open space filled to the brim with tall fabric banners, ornamental pillows bunched in corners, spidery hanging hammocks—and in an alcove, dresses in rows on blond wooden hangers. All in wild colors. Everything, including the dresses, bore outlandish and vivid colors never before encountered in daily life. Colors from a child's paint box! Colors from the tropics! Nor were these new colors sitting static on the dresses but instead were pulsating in bands next to each other or undulating in prints of amoebic blobs or exploding into huge flowers.

Not only that. Up close the dresses were not cinched or tight but cut like primitive paper-doll frocks, which meant *no girdles were necessary.* They were made of heavy cotton canvas, like flags, and each dress was different. Each seemed to be sending its own flag message from some effortlessly happy place.

And all the places were Finland.

Little did B. know that Finland was famous for dour

people, snow and ice, homicides, suicides, and grim unquenchable *sisu* (stubborn courage in adversity).

But also for short summers overflowing with light. Armi Ratia, the impresario of the Marimekko clothes, was an internal refugee from the eastern part of Finland called Karelia, which had been lost to Stalin in World War II. Armi Ratia once said that when Karelia was lost, summer had stayed behind there.

Now summer was revived, by means of the dresses.

Me, I was enchanted, taken back to a time outside of time, to a place apart from the known world, where primeval dresses were singing all by themselves.

And B. was paralyzed by desire, not just for the dresses but for their aura. If you were a woman back then in Cambridge, Mass., and not an academic drone, you had to have a Marimekko dress. Jamie had two; Ellen, a copy of one; Ronnie didn't have one since she "went for the Jackie Kennedy look." But even Jackie Kennedy had seven Marimekkos, as reported by *Sports Illustrated,* which put a picture of her wearing one in a motorboat next to a tousled-haired JFK on its cover.

B. circled the Marimekko dresses for half a year. She stood among them and shifted each hanger with a glassy-eyed stare. She saved every waitressing dollar she could put away. Then she bought one: a straight-down tube whose top half featured pink sea-urchin things printed on rust-colored canvas, while the bottom featured rust sea urchins on pink. The tube had a mandarin collar with three pointed brass buttons ascending the right side.

The pink-and-rust dress had meant so much and cost so much that B. wore it only on precious and worthy occasions. It sat in her closet paralyzed by her adoration, which I thought stupid. Then came a sudden windfall: another girl down her hall (not one of the four but well heeled too) found that *her* Marimekko of black-and-white zigzags didn't quite fit, so passed it to B.

I was a two-Marimekko wardrobe! How proud I was. About that time, B. went home for spring vacation and took both of the Marimekkos. She had already begun a rescue operation on the mother's attention-starved wardrobe. From Germany she'd brought the mother a baby blue T-shirt with a low neck, which looked awful on its new owner because its color was a young color, meant for thin young arms, a fact B. only half realized.

Now she impulsively gave the mother the original pink-and-rust Marimekko. I was upset about this, but B., who'd just gotten an A on an English paper, judged the black-and-white with zigzags the more sophisticated of the two.

The mother was delighted with the pink-and-rust dress. She had always liked bright colors and was then trying to win civil rights in our city by acts of civil disobedience. She wore it a lot. It looked bold on her and good.

But all too soon B. would get it back.

By 1968, I was drastically changed. I'd grown lewd, audacious, and happy. A provocative mood was in the air of the college, and B. finally felt she belonged.

This could all be seen in one dress, a navy-and-white polka-dotted mini-dress with a white pointy collar, a shiny white belt, and a short flippy skirt. It was a ridiculous dress. The white dots were not discreet little dots but big cartoon-like discs, and the skirt was almost nil. But this dress absorbed all the hopes of B.'s body-in-love, physical hopes that swept even uneasy Me into a moment of illusory exaltation.

The moment came in the library, where B. sat in the high-ceilinged Reading Room wearing the polka-dot dress, with thighs ultra-crossed (the skirt was so short), thinking about the elevator, which at any time could be taken up three floors to a room housing the books of a small rare-books collection. Up there, babysitting the rare books, sat a graduate student section leader. He was from Texas. He had a twangy accent, a mini-pompadour, a fervent manner, and a distracted smile. B., in her seat down in the Reading Room, spent a lot of time devising a really plausible question that she could go up in the elevator to ask him.

"Could you remind me which of the Prescott histories alludes most directly to Andrew Jackson?"

Once B. was upstairs, the dress, with its pointy white collar and its short skating skirt, shone in the dark on the edge of the pool of light made by a brass reading lamp on the desk, where the Texas graduate student sat, looking up edgily from his book. B. ignored the edginess because she believed the skirt was blotting out her own unsightly hips and stomach and tops of thighs and giving her a shape that was perfect. And this sensation of perfection, welling up from a body that seemed to have turned both taut and ripe for this occasion, overrode all doubts.

B. always believed it was I, as the dress, who prompted the graduate student to call, when he did call. He asked B. to a concert. B. rushed into the Common Room on her floor to tell everyone he had called. Glad faces were raised from books.

B. went to that concert wearing the polka-dotted dress, then home to the grad student's rented room on a seedy Cambridge street. She stayed the night. Some days later he called again and asked her to a party at someone's rented house. It was cold; B. wore the checked suit skirt and tights. But the grad student drank a lot at the party, and on the way home, skidding on the ice with his arm in B.'s, he told her that he couldn't feel much at that moment since he was "on the rebound" from someone else.

Even now I have to pause and take a breath. The shock, the internal cry of pain, the heart snapping shut, as B. skidded along the ice with her arm in the arm of the betrayer. That eager heart of B.'s, battered by the father's carelessness, emboldened by Me to beat ardently inside the polka-dot dress, had shut up tight like a clamshell.

Despite that shock, the affair went on for a while. B. stayed overnight sometimes in the section leader's rundown room that smelled of sleep. The two of them might have grown gently closer if subsequent events hadn't put B. out of the reach of his embarrassed kindness.

As for me—maybe I once *had* had the power, embodied in the polka-dotted dress, to cause that young Texan to call. But I couldn't open B.'s heart again to him. The slap of those words had left a deep mark. Still, and this is the point—I thrill to the memory of the loud polka-dot dress. It was present at the moment when B. and I first caught fire together.

The great poet Cavafy wrote, "Body, remember not only how much you were loved . . . but also those desires for you / that glowed plainly in the eyes." He could have written "*Wardrobe,* remember not only how much you were loved . . . ," or better still, "how much you *hoped* you were loved . . ."

Hope is all that We wardrobes need, in order to become—I hate this word but it's the right one here—empowered.

n a little midwestern mall, in a back corner of a big fluorescent-lit store, B. found a sleeveless black nylon dress with a skirt to mid-thigh, which buttoned up the front with small pearly buttons and tied at the waist with a thin black sash. The nylon was a soft filmy kind, for once not masquerading as cotton, which made the skirt sit correctly on B.'s hips.

It was for the mother's funeral.

B. had come home for spring vacation of 1969. It was a month after the icy night of the grad student's rebuff. From home, the family had headed off south on Highway 61 for the sea coast of Alabama—a surprise trip arranged by the mother. B. was driving the car, the mother was sitting beside her, and all the brothers and sisters were in the back. The accident involved a lot of rain, a passing truck, and the wall of a bridge. The mother broke her neck in the passenger seat.

Don't ask Me what B. was wearing in the car or what the mother or the kids were wearing because I can't remember. B. had a concussion. Maybe concussions erase the memories even of wardrobes.

But I can recall My first thought on arriving at the hospital where they pronounced the mother dead: "We have nothing black." No black in a female wardrobe—that's hard to believe. Back then it was normal. Pastels dominated most female wardrobes. The masses of black in women's closets would come later.

One of the mother's friends, with a wry smile and a slow-talking manner, took B. to find a black dress. She didn't say, "At a time like this just get anything that fits." She said, "Make sure you get something you like."

Everyone who came to the house saw the black nylon dress, because B. wore it when she opened the door. The father was too broken up to answer the door. The overflow crowd at the funeral saw the dress too, since B., the siblings, and the father all in new black clothes entered from a side door in front of the church after everyone was assembled.

In fact I, as the black nylon dress, *became* B. for months. I had to. There wasn't any B. Inside she was careening back and forth between excesses of love for everyone and flashes of horror, even as she went through the mourning motions. No other sensations came to her but these—though sometimes, like a quiet voice from the real world (Me), came the mundane sensation of wearing the black dress.

What I mean is that B. returned periodically to sanity through checking how the dress felt next to her skin. How fortunate, went the loop of thought inside B., that that mall had turned up a dress that was short but not mini, funereal but not pompous, and filmy to the touch. And how convenient that it was lightweight and could travel, so it wouldn't have to be just a death dress. It could be "drowned" in a sink, squeezed out, and dried overnight wrinkleless like the drip-dry skirt, a prospect that promised a kind of sensory pleasure for Me, and eventually for B. when some time had gone by.

It was her first black dress.

B. went back to Harvard a week after the accident, back to concerned friends and the newly tender though hesitant graduate student. Before leaving she took the pink-and-rust Marimekko out of the mother's closet without asking anyone, and put it in her own suitcase. It had been hers, after all. And the mother had really loved it, so it would make a bright wearable memorial.

The rest of the mother's clothes B. didn't take or even look at. They weren't compatible with the rest of Me. But since then she has had regrets and so have I. I would like at this point to have a clearer memory of My earliest role model, even if I was still a little scornful back then.

As far as B. knows the mother's clothes just hung in her closet for about seven months until the father got married and was persuaded by the new stepmother to move himself and the remaining siblings into her chic renovated townhouse in the downtown bohemian part of the city. At that point everything in the grand old rundown house in the suburbs had to be sold. The stepmother, eager to discard the funereal atmosphere, brought in a B'nai Brith committee to hold the sale. B. learned from the sister that the mother's old leather purse had been sold, still with a bloodstain on it.

B. was on the road in Europe so didn't see the clothes again.

Later a few things trickled down to her (and Me), probably through that little sister. In B.'s scarf drawer today is a scarf the mother wore a lot: red silk with white polka dots, though it's so old the white dots are now ragged holes. B. can't throw it away.

In B.'s jewelry drawer is the mother's chunky gold charm bracelet worn for parties. The charms are: a gold dollar from 1899, a gold four-leaf clover from the mother's twentieth birthday, just before she married, and a gold disc engraved with the date of her sister's wedding, June 3, 1953. B. also got the mother's antique Zuni sunburst turquoise-and-silver earrings (screw-ons; the mother hadn't pierced her own ears) but they disappeared, stolen probably by a young woman with writing aspirations who once stayed in B.'s apartment while she was gone. And the best thing she got: the mother's pink-gold ring set with a black pearl. But *it* got lost almost right away, years before the Zuni sun-bursts disappeared. Losing that ring made B. sob so hard she scared herself.

Jewelry is sometimes the most human part of Me.

But for the record, and as an exercise in remembering, I'm enumerating here some other lost items, which in her numbness after the accident B. failed to keep track of. The camel-colored wool polo coat the mother wore, and the old fur-trimmed galoshes she pulled over her shoes for Christmas caroling in the neighborhood with B. and the siblings, maybe her favorite activity. The maroon wool hood cut like a knight's hood to show the face (her eager face with the wide mouth), which she put over her head on the coldest Christmases. A soft charcoal wool dress with a button-up polo top, which she always brightened up with the red polka-dot scarf at the neck and a red belt at the waist. A tent-shaped red wool coat with a self-tie at the neck that she'd bought near the end of her life, when everyone told her she *had* to get a new coat. Her olive green Bermuda shorts, her old white tennis shoes, her white shirt with a Peter Pan collar . . .

Really the mother, even after six children, had a good and youthful figure.

And she wore the classic Chanel No. 5 all her life, but only for parties.

After the accident B. and I were very much to-gether, because B. was very much alone.

She graduated from college in a procession on the quadrangle lawn attended by the father, looking politely haunted, plus an anxiously affectionate aunt (the oldest of the three, not the middle one), and the paternal grandparents.

Graduation severs anyone from four years of college life, and in B.'s case her earlier home was gone too. She fled from impending grief by taking a job that sent her to Europe. It sounded glamorous. It was for a U.S. travel company with branch offices in Paris, Rome, and London, for which B. was supposed to research youth tour packages—even if the bosses, when they flew to Europe for meetings, didn't treat her like a young colleague but more like a lone female to sidle up to and invite to their rooms.

It could be that B. brought such lascivious treatment on herself through overeagerness of manner. But she didn't care because she still wasn't quite present in her body. I was still representing her.

Even so I barely remember the office clothes she wore to work in those European capitals, though I have no trouble remembering the after-work clothes she hid from the bosses, even more than regular office inhabitants hide their leisure clothes from their bosses.

B. called them the secret clothes. They were supposed to help her become an invisible stranger, hidden in plain sight in the streets of European cities, moving with the flow of humanity and yet against it, at one with the crowd yet not of it. That's how she saw things then. After work in the branch office of whatever city B. found herself in, she would return to her hotel and change into the secret clothes. Then she (and I) would go out onto the city streets and walk for hours.

The secret clothes were the clothes of the students of whatever city it was. In Rome, B. bought a shimmery orange fitted shirt that looked Roman, because back home, shirts were not fitted, nor did they come in interesting or vibrant colors (in those days America was mostly a place of muddy maroons and virtuous plaids). Italian girls wore these fitted shirts with A-line skirts and slingbacks, so B. also bought an A-line navy blue skirt of light wool and navy slingback heels. Dressed after work in her Italian clothes, she would pause in her room, staring down from the hotel window onto a bridge lined with big white Mussolini-era statues until the statues turned blue in the twilight. Then she would go down to the Piazza Navona, with its curvy fountain basins and mobs of tourists, and take twilight pictures of lit-up statues and lit-up water.

B. liked looking at mobs of tourists, especially if she thought they couldn't tell where *she* was from. "At the center of the world, yet hidden from it," said Baudelaire.

In Paris she bought mint green thin-wale corduroy pants, which were soft. France was then the country of different-colored corduroy pants. One day B. got a sore throat in her Paris hotel, which was a crumbling eighteenth-century city chateau the bosses were thinking of buying, so had planted her there "undercover." Getting sick alone in a strange country was unsettling. An old lady down the hall recommended very hot tea with rum, so B. drank some and got into bed wearing the mint green corduroy pants, and woke up many hours later in the blue twilight with the flu gone, lifted—and the sound of two Mozart violins weaving together on her radio and the curlicue grills on her balcony making Mozartian shapes, and the mint-greenness of the rumpled pants Mozartian too.

All was not Mozartian, though, the day B. lay down

in the seedy massage clinic in the hotel courtyard to try out the aging masseur. She relaxed until he began to unzip the green pants, and although what he was doing felt good, she lurched up and shouted at him.

B. in the light green pants left France for England on the boat train, since the bosses had called her back there. On the windy boat deck she met a French girl of twelve, Sophie, with a lot of tangled black hair, who was wearing red corduroy pants. Sophie was with her school class but seemed for a moment to need the attention of a lone adult like B. So the two stood apart from the others, talking at the railing, in tomato red and mint green corduroys.

n London in the fall, the bosses halted B. for several months to help out in the branch office of that city. She found a room in a large, white high-ceilinged Kensington flat with three British girls, each with a room of her own, none of whom she ever saw except for the main girl called Sydney. Now that she had an address, she wrote a few letters back to the Texas grad student in Cambridge, and got a few wanly affectionate letters from him.

And because the flat was near Biba, she found Biba.

Everyone in London knew Biba except B., who passed it by chance one evening on the Kensington High Street as the air was getting colder. She saw the tendrily name printed in gold on the shop window and just went in, or fell in. Inside, Biba was vast and dark except for spotlights on potted palms, mirrors, clothes racks, and antique dressers piled high with sweaters and jewelry and feathers. The floor was made of wooden planks, I think, or at least was uneven.

What was this place? The cavern that Aladdin tumbled into? A treasure chamber in an old palace?

A young woman named Barbara Hulanicki had dreamed it up. This Polish-born wizard was perhaps more important to clothes even than the more famous Mary Quant, because she'd put a whiff of nostalgia into them, though not of the woozy kind. Hippie clothes up to then had been inexact about the past, which they posited as a dreamy utopia lost in the wilds of history. Hulanicki focused her Biba clothes, through allusions to utopias precisely imagined by artists and designers: glints of the shimmering palettes of Camelot and the Lady of the Lake, of the pre-Raphaelite medieval, of the Flapper-era Byzantine. All these magically serious allusions bombarded B. as she stood paralyzed with longing that first time in the store.

To Me, Biba felt like an amusement park for wardrobes. I was enchanted, even as I felt B. slipping into anonymity.

Evening after evening she wandered around Biba and became Nobody except for ghostlike skin and a mouth making an O in the mirror. She fingered everything. She let the feathers brush her. She couldn't buy anything because she'd become frightened of buying. It was a new phobia, having to do with despair masquerading as exuberance, having to do with the sense that no one from her old life would ever find her in the nighttime spotlit cave of Biba.

This was the bottom of the grief pit for B., the first of the bottoms. You might say she evaporated in Biba, in the scary ritual of losing, then finding, then losing herself in the guise of an ever-changing image in a mirror.

Finally I grabbed her and insisted that she buy *something* in the store, so she came away with a slinky ribbed thing in a mulberry color. It clung so and was so skinny in the shoulders when she buttoned it that you couldn't call it a cardigan. More like mulberry-colored chain mail.

And what did Biba add to My inner self? Never-before-encountered colors like *aubergine, cobalt, slate gray.* They were the notes in each color range that glowed for a moment, on their way down to black.

$\bigvee\bigvee$inter, fog, rain, and damp came to London, so B. in her first impulse of practicality said we had to go to an army-navy store. I resisted. I thought this meant army green, camouflage, and Vietnam. But the store turned up something unexpected: a coat from the *Swedish* army, which was white, or whitish, made of heavy sheepskin, skin side out, with a tendrily white sheep's fur collar and huge white buttons that closed the coat with canvas tabs.

It was a little dirty but warm. To B. it seemed the bearer of an important message delivered, by chance, as if from the *I Ching*—something like "hello!" from the Swedish soldier whose coat it had been, before it was parted from him and sent randomly through the byways of the world.

This coat was the only item of the secret clothes

that the bosses saw. B. wore it to meetings, because she needed to get to the meetings in a coat and she had no other. The bosses had never encountered anything like it. One swore he saw it move as it stood in the corner of a meeting room. It could stand by itself.

The coat was beautiful in a rough way. At least it looked right when B. went to a London movie house to see *Easy Rider,* about big elongated motorcycles on the sunny highways of home. Everybody in the London *Easy Rider* audience was shaggy.

I also loved the coat because to Me it said "protection." It was a caricature of protection. And protection was what I wanted to give B. at that moment when she herself wasn't corporeal but was more or less a phantom seeking an evanescent shape in Me.

In that coat someone could ride in an open truck or live on the streets, or at least photograph the streets at all times, which is what B. thought she wanted to do, instead of holding down a job in a bourgeois travel company.

B. thought she wanted to live in an empty white room embellished only by black-and-white photographs taken by her, photographs of streets, that she would hang on the walls.

B. abruptly quit the travel company and prepared to leave London for home. Her last London purchase was a pair of blue-and-brown striped denim bell-bottoms of a plush cotton that gave the illusion of warmth. She said she would never dress up again and the bell-bottoms would have to serve for every occasion.

It was because of another movie, *Zabriskie Point,* whose young West Coast heroine for most of the story was semi-involved with a corporate sugar daddy, an unstraightforward situation that caused, at the film's end, the slow-motion explosion of a corporate conference center in California's sunny, empty Death Valley. Also the shaggy English boy in the next seat at the movie told B. that no one needed anything to get through life because "Need is an auto-induced mechanism implanted by the corporate culture that unfortunately permeates our innermost thoughts."

Among B.'s confused impulses then was one to try to shut Me out, to divest herself of Me and our joint history. She said again that she needed to live an empty life in a white room, with no extra clothes. So she left all the beautiful secret clothes behind when we flew out of London, stashed away in the luggage rooms of different hotels, where they might still be.

It was a shock that she could decimate Me, seemingly without a care in the world.

Back in our midwestern city, the striped bell-bottoms, rumpled by now, were a hit with the younger siblings because their high school crowd was also wearing striped bell-bottoms. A skinny friend of the siblings presented B. with a dark brown leather hat to go with the pants. It had a wide brim encircled with braided rawhide.

This outfit was strange and evasive in My opinion. A mildly drunk woman guest of the soon-to-be step-mother described B., wearing it, as "either a young person dressed like an old person or an old person dressed like a young person."

Sometimes I tried tempting B. with an outfit other than the bell-bottoms and the hat—like a flowing dress or normal jeans—but she told Me to shut up because "These striped pants are the Traveling Costume, and Life is a Journey."

After the father's wedding in which the drip-dry blue skirt did faithful service one last time, B. in the bell-bottoms and hat traveled back east with the graduate student from the library. Now with a beard and a midsection, he had driven out to pick B. up and bring her to the college town where he had his first job as a professor, so she could audition for faculty wife.

He was patient and gentle. He suggested that B. might think about applying to grad school at his college and studying the books she loved. But B. didn't have much to say to him. She withdrew from the faculty parties and went into spare rooms to sleep on piles of guests' coats. Anyway, faculty wives can't wear only striped bell-bottoms and a leather hat, day after day, to parties and concerts.

A few weeks later B., in the bell-bottoms and hat, flew home again to the Midwest and, a week after that, in the same costume, headed off in the other direction, west, in an old beat-up Mercedes ("beat-up" in hippie language canceled "Mercedes"), with a new acquaintance who was the nephew of the new stepmother.

What was B. seeking? A new life in an empty white room. A life that was "organic," clean, and free of bour-

geois pretensions and bourgeois ties to lost or recon-
figured families. Also a reunion with the college roommate who had rented a house in Berkeley and had
started a new life herself.

I, much diminished, came along in the new red
nylon, four-tiered backpack that was now B.'s luggage,
as we crossed Oklahoma, New Mexico, and Arizona
(B. fell in love with Navajo silver) and drove right into
the bell-bottoms' spiritual home: the landscape of
Death Valley.

n Berkeley, California, in 1970, cardboard boxes of clothes sat on street corners, so anyone could trade an old garment for another old garment.

B. got a dress out of one of them, faded thin-wale dark blue corduroy to the knees, with long skinny sleeves and no waist except many small gathers under the bust. Because the dress had surfaced in the street box, the bell-bottoms got put away, though not dropped like fair trade into the box. B. couldn't bring herself to do that, so she put them in the back of the roommate's closet in the rented house in Berkeley.

B. thought to add some ornamentation to the dress, which was very plain. Furious at herself for having resisted the mother's attempts to teach her to sew, she got a large needle and some pink yarn and wrote, in primitive jags, the refrain of the old Shaker hymn then being sung at alternative gatherings, such as the New Education Conference she'd been to on a mountain near Berkeley: "When true simplicity is gained / To bow and to bend we will not be ashamed." For a week this wisdom writ wildly in pink yarn adorned the dress's bodice. Then the dress went into the room-mate's washing machine and came out broadcasting gibberish, or saying in hippie-speak, "I bear a secret message known only to the wearer."

The dress with its pink gibberish is superimposed in memory on a variety of California landscapes: the white houses of Berkeley streets where B. walked and walked; the on-ramps of Berkeley superhighways where she hitchhiked from; the palm trees on Santa Barbara's main drag where she hitchhiked to; the white-linoleum police station in Oakland where she was taken for shoplifting a piece of cheese; the green-brown coastal cliffs of Point Reyes National Park where she swallowed an LSD pill and saw those same cliffs change to yellow and purple and start to pulsate.

To complete B.'s portrait in those days, add hiking boots, thick white socks, and a rubbery down jacket of navy blue made by a just-born Berkeley company called The North Face, located in a mud-surrounded gray-wood warehouse, where the band Creedence Clearwater Revival also practiced. A casual midwestern friend of B.'s who was into gear (they were all casual friends; they were all into gear) said that the jacket would be all B. would ever need in life.

I was getting tired of "all you'll ever need in life."

But though the dress, with its accessories of jacket and boots, now shut out any items of clothing except itself, I didn't hate it like I'd hated the bell-bottoms. It reminded Me of Marimekko—essence of dress—yet it was also a found object that fate had sent to B. at no cost, plus it was redolent of Appalachia and poor women on sagging porches. The note of "poor" was a necessary ingredient in whatever style was being born on the streets of Berkeley. The note of "woman" struck Me as a good sign about B.'s state of grief and recovery.

It's true that she had thrown herself headfirst into the hippie dream of riding the rails or the equivalent, like the young hoboes of the 1930s. But now at least she was calling on Me to portray her as something other than a blurred-gender, hat-shaded, indeterminate being who wasn't really anybody. The dress, the jacket, the boots and socks alluded more or less consciously to a mixture of the old and the new, the homespun and the technological, the aggressive and the demure, the boy-like and girl-like.

In My slow and halting rebirth after the bell-bottoms debacle, these disparate elements would be the ones I would use to try to forge, slowly, fitfully, painfully—desperately—a new bond with B.

B. left the West because of linger-
ing terror from the Point Reyes
LSD trip and went back east, to
enroll in the Harvard School of Education. The ghost of the mother had
sent B. back there, since the mother, when alive, had
said many times that teaching was "a safe career." But
before school started, B. met up with two now-grown
little brothers and drove in one brother's old car to visit
the paternal grandparents in their New Hampshire
farmhouse turned retirement home.

It was a hot day. The house, white with black shutters, stood on a rise above a dirt road. A red barn
stood beside it. From house and barn stretched meadows on all sides, and beyond the meadows rose blue
mountains.

The grandparents emerged from the house as B.

and the brothers drove up. The grandfather wore a neat plaid shirt tucked into some brown pleated pants belted high around his ample middle; the grandmother, a crisp blue linen sundress with rickrack on the straps and skirt, seamed stockings, and her old, neat high-heeled shoes. She was still tall and thin. Over the linen sundress was a gardening apron from whose pocket stuck a green trowel.

Even with gardening implements, even in the country mode, they were the same. Unfortunately for them, B. and the brothers were not, since their clothes bore no relation to the sartorial profiles the grandparents had long wished for in grandchildren. The siblings had decided to climb a mountain, so emerged from the car wearing old jeans from secondhand bins, old jeans shirts, bandanas tied around their heads and threaded through their belt loops, and old army green canvas-covered water bottles slung over their shoulders, together with lumpy book bags. B. hefted the four-tiered red backpack, now battered and torn, filled with sweaters, flashlights, and brown rice.

The generations faced each other for several seconds. Then the older, with grim smiles, invited the younger inside. All trooped to the living room with its exquisitely simple Shaker furniture bought at country auctions, its primitive paintings of clipper ships on choppy seas. The young contingent sipped clear 7-Up;

the old one sipped amber highballs; all nibbled thin pretzel sticks from a tall handblown glass jar with a peaked glass top and chatted guardedly.

Through the window B. admired the grandmother's garden. Purple irises and yellow pansies rimmed a grassy space bordered by a low stone wall, with the backdrop of blue mountains. The flowers looked happy in the sunlit chill air, but when B. attempted to tell the grandmother this, the old lady gave a slight nod and looked down her nose.

The next day the band of B. and brothers set off on their three-day trek armed with a cleansing diet of brown rice, though, since B. burned all the rice over a campfire the first night, they actually subsisted on the unclean Spam and peanut butter left miraculously in a lean-to by a group from Yale.

Back at the grandparents' in wrinkled clothes, the three were met with the same guarded manner. B. finally asked, "What's wrong?"

"It's difficult for your grandmother," said the grandfather, "to understand why you children can't travel with proper luggage."

I have remembered the remark because I had always admired the paternal grandparents' large matching light beige suitcases with squeaky leather hinges, also their smaller pigskin-leather case that, when opened, revealed two whisky bottles securely strapped in, two strapped-in shot glasses, four tall drinking glasses, and two pewter swizzle sticks. In one compact case were assembled all the accoutrements needed to set up a bar wherever the grandparents landed.

Now, with their petulant remark, I changed My mind and became almost proud of B.'s battered four-tiered red backpack and her lumpy book bag.

ducation school started in the summer of 1970. At that time, even a bigwig bulwark like Harvard was hosting alternative-thought currents, such as Sensitivity Training for aspiring teachers.

The Sensitivity instructor, a red-haired, monkey-faced ex-dancer from Canada who wore sailor jeans before anyone else, liked to turn off the lights so students could "let out aggression" in violent improvisation. One day he changed tactics and told them to sit quietly on the floor, close their eyes, then open them and start to read: their own autobiographies.

That's when B. surprised herself by discovering, on the first page—Me—in the form of the small clean red overalls. In Europe she'd clung feverishly to Me by means of the secret clothes, then pushed Me away with the didactic bell-bottoms. Now, suddenly, all un-bidden, she rediscovered Me. This was the first time after the accident she'd thought of Me quietly. And thought of home.

B. read on in the imaginary book (which bears some resemblance to the book you have in your hands). She was still in the bedroom holding the red overalls. She put them down on the floor and took out underpants and a short-sleeved white T-shirt from a higher drawer. She put these on, leaving the three buttons up to the neck of the T-shirt unbuttoned because she couldn't do that yet. Then she put on the red overalls, whose buttons at shoulder level she just managed to fit into the metal tabs on the straps.

Dressed in clean clothes, the B. in the imaginary book went outside (no one else was awake) to the ter-race bordered by the big oak, where birds sang in the new light and the moss-covered bricks were cool on her bare feet.

Inspired by the monkey-faced Sensitivity teacher, B. decided to try a dance class, modern dance this time. She'd tried drawing earlier but hadn't managed to do a good drawing of the class's first still-life object, a motorcycle. The instructor had laughed at her because the engine in her drawing didn't look like it would work.

She left drawing and went over to the old redbrick women's gym on grassy Radcliffe Yard. The Radcliffe Gym was an art-nouveau cum Colonial Revival brick building with a soaring second floor, taller than its first floor. Inside the front door in the hall, a small barefoot woman with long, loose black hair and sharp black eyes like a little animal's was hurrying along holding a tambourine-shaped drum and a mallet. She wore a navy blue leotard and navy footless tights. "Class is starting," she told B. "No dance clothes? Go look. Box in my office . . ."

Another old clothes box! Out of which came My next incarnation: torn black footless tights and a too-tight long-sleeved plum leotard. On the upper floor of the gym, under the high raftered wooden ceiling, two drummers sat on a small stage; below them on the floor the sharp-eyed woman in navy blue, with her own drum, faced two rows of barefooted tights-and-leotarded students. A lumpy B. crept behind the second row. High windows cast light on the polished floor. "Pliés," said the woman. "And *one!*" she hit the drum.

In this tableau, I, as the cast-off tights and leotard, did not look quite right. But B. was in motion; that was what mattered. I'd been waiting for her to move. Thanks to her old ballet debacle, B. knew a little how to bend her knees in plié, stretch a foot out in *tendu,* move across the floor on a phrase of *down up up, down up up.* And indeed, in this high-raftered upper hall of the gym that became for a while the center of B.'s life, her physicality would return to her, drop by drop, which would bring Me relief.

Without a body sending Me signals, I can't live. Like Tinkerbell, bodies, not just minds, have to wish their wardrobes awake.

Besides this, the timing was right. B.'s body was jump-starting, just when the idea of body-moving-freely-in-clothes had hit the whole of cutting-edge fashion. Dance was the key, or rather dance clothes, tight but non-binding, which meant stretchy. Stretchy was born then (with Lycra, invented in 1959). Rudi Gernreich of the tight tube dresses and Mary Quant, of the miniskirts and the liberated (from girdles) pantyhose, had taken inspiration from dance clothes.

Dance clothes had meant liberation ever since late-eighteenth-century ballerinas Camargo and Sallé had shortened dancing skirts and discarded petticoats. But the circus was the real source of modern dancing's skin-tight garments. In 1859, a twenty-year-old Toulouse-born athlete, Jules Léotard, joined the Cirque Napoleon and invented the Flying Trapeze, as well as a costume for it, a close-fitted knitted silk thing that sheathed arms, legs, and torso. The mustachioed and bubble-coiffed Léotard had posed cockily in photos in this silky second skin, holding the end of a trapeze swing, with a little skirt covering his private parts and thin lace-up boots on his feet.

After fifty years the leotard lost its legs and became a torso sheath for athletes, helped by the bravado of swim star Annette Kellerman, who got arrested on a Boston beach in 1907 for wearing a one-piece swimsuit.

As for the tights—they'd been around, as "hose," since burly Renaissance men had shown off their legs in multicolored leg casings. And dancers had long worn cotton-knit tights like long johns for rehearsal warmth. In the 1950s, thanks to Martha Graham's stretch fabrics and George Balanchine's stripped-down bodies, stage tights came into their own. In 1959 they hit city streets, when Allen Gant, Sr., of North Carolina's Glen Raven Mills (descendant of John Gant, the Mills' founder) reinvented them in stretch nylon and called them, with sly innuendo, pantyhose.

But even after the newfangled pantyhose had zoomed across the ocean to Piccadilly and back again, they stayed infused with the aura of dance. Pantyhose à la Mary Quant meant a kicking of legs, a leaping in the street, even a flying on the high trapeze. Pantyhose and tights were one and the same (except some had no feet). They were motion! And I'd gotten a double jolt of motion—from the leotard and tights B. took from the box that day at the gym.

Too big a jolt. After just a few weeks of dance, B. started planning everything around those classes. She said she felt right only in that high-raftered dancing hall with its polished floor. She said *space* was a dancer's clothing.

It sounded flowery but wasn't very nice for Me to hear. Also I became dizzy, with clothes coming off and going on her all day in the rush back and forth between school and dancing.

That's the two-edged sword of dance. We wardrobes

of dancers get these wonderful sinewy bodies to dress, and B.'s was getting more sinewy by the day. Yet often the bodies don't care. Or they stop caring.

It is My experience that the possibility of getting lost haunts all dancers—getting lost in motion. They need never stop and be human (and wear real clothes) again.

The dance teacher invited students to her elegant old city apartment after B. and several others had gotten degrees. She greeted the students in a Bedouin dress of faded navy blue with vertical magenta stripes and embroidery on the bodice.

In her living room, red and black pots from New Mexico sat on a shelf, sacred rocks covered every surface from windowsills to tables, two gray cats with yellow eyes slinked about, and a green stained-glass mask hung in a bay window. The teacher fed the students brown rice and vegetables with *gomasi* sprinkled on, crushed sesame seeds and sea salt.

B. decided to become macrobiotic too and embrace the scale of Yin and Yang, on which sugar and meat occupied the far ends but brown rice was the perfect item in the middle. Actually she decided to eat only brown rice *crackers* because, during days of substitute-teaching and dancing, she had no time to cook the rice.

She also badly wanted a Bedouin dress, and one day, in a Cambridge backstreet, she came upon a small shop in front of which, outside on the sidewalk, a row of such dresses hung on a clothes rack. All of them were faded navy blue with vertical magenta stripes; all smelled like old sunlight; each had a different pattern cross-stitched on its square-cut bodice.

A chorus of dresses, all authentic. At that moment I, in the guise of the blue corduroy dress with pink gibberish, which B. happened to be wearing, felt cosmically impertinent. These dresses had been worn by authentic Bedouin women out there in the desert. The embroidery on the bodices was not some frivolous hippie message but part of *the pattern of their lives.* The cloth alone, that worn dark blue and magenta, brought hallucinations of distant horizons, relentless sun, precious water in a copper ladle.

And the designs on the bodices . . . each had once marked out a separate woman in that harsh landscape.

B. didn't have the money but decided she must have a Bedouin dress, so she bought one, using her first credit card. The dress had densely sewn red and green crosses on the bodice. Red and green against blue and magenta broke the rules of taste and color. When she slipped the dress over her head (no zipper or buttons) it felt cool on her aching muscles. She glided around in it at home, trying out a nomadic walk that could be used to cross a desert.

The idea had been for the Bedouin dress to replace the corduroy dress as the everyday costume, but in the end B. didn't wear it that much. It didn't look right in New England streets sporting dirty patches of snow. Also she felt obscurely guilty. Had the woman who'd worn the dress wanted to let it go?

But I was able to absorb a Bedouin note into My accumulating identity. That is, I became aware, through that dress, of previously unknown colors, shapes, and ornamentations, which came from so-called primitive societies actually wiser than ours, wiser about the relations between clothes and wearers.

I learned about a universe of sorrow and loss from the Bedouin dress. I learned about the cycle of precious clothes being lost to people and found by other people—perhaps people who didn't know the real value of a wardrobe.

Consumed by dance and subsisting on brown rice crackers, B. grew thin and weak. One day, while walking on the street, she fell prey to a hallucination of blood swimming before her eyes. She held on to a tree. The next day the doctor said it was pneumonia. The dance teacher took her into her city apartment and installed her on her couch, near any number of the sacred rocks, and lent her an old soft bathrobe made of quilted pink satin, still partly shiny.

The borrowed bathrobe showed Me what maturity for a wardrobe might look like. It took sinuous shapes as B. shifted positions on the couch. It smelled of an almost imperceptible perfume. Ordinarily I would have felt weird getting mixed up with someone else's wardrobe, but not then, because of how absorbed B.

was in the music she was listening to, while lying immobile on the couch for a month.

The teacher was at the gym all day, but as she left she would put a stack of records on the record player. Billie Holiday sang, "Ooo Ooo Ooo, what a little moonlight can do"; Connee Boswell sang, "Humming to Myself"; Mildred Bailey sang, "All of me, why not take all of me?" Cocooned in the pink robe, B. listened to these voices from a ghostly past, singing about comfort, about how one needs it and never gets it. She was transfixed. She had never heard this music. Dylan, Janis, Stevie Winwood, et al., had blotted it out.

And how like the old jazz was the pink robe, which contained some kind of history too, not just the dance teacher's history but the history of women who'd looked out of windows and turned on radios and lived in their bathrobes when they'd needed to.

The history held within it a new idea of home, not a house in the suburbs like the one B. had come from, but a room in the city among millions of rooms (millions of lit-up windows), where you could curl up and long for things and wear a bathrobe that wasn't a traveling costume.

Every day B. staggered into the teacher's bathroom, put her face down by the faucet and a towel over her head so she could breathe in steam and cough. The doctor had said to do this. One day the skipping and itching inside her lungs stopped, as if a high wind had blown her onto a quiet beach. It was a cold day, but sun streamed in through the windows. She regarded herself in the old full-length mirror on the bathroom door. Pale and greenish, with the bumps of hipbones visible through the smoothed-down pink robe. Oh joy! Very thin.

How stupid to want to look sick when one is well. That's how B. was then, a muddle-headed dancer. Worse than muddle-headed—doom eager, as Martha Graham would have said (without irony or alarm). But not in her whole self. It's true that some part of B. wanted to subsist on air and become a skeleton upon which I could hang—never tight, always loose.

But another part veered away from this heroic ideal.

When B. went back to her own almost-empty apartment, the dance teacher kept the robe, which had "been with me so long," but gave B. instead an assortment of scarves that she said was going to Goodwill anyway. B. draped the scarves on top of her dresser; she could see them from the kitchen countertop where she dutifully ate thick soups to strengthen herself. One scarf was green and blue chiffon; one, shimmering orange silk; and one, black matte silk imprinted with a mysterious green-and-mustard-colored fish in a crackly batik pattern.

The scarves gave Me an extra role, in home decor.

But they worked even better on the street, knotted at B.'s neck, speaking in regular wardrobese (referring faintly to the jousts and tournaments of yore). Every time B. went out she knotted one at her neck to protect herself from pneumonia. That's when I learned the secret of scarves. If they're tied with a belief in their protective powers they will look right.

Everyone will ask to be taught how to tie a scarf.

And the life of the scarf's wearer will revive itself by means of such small acts of self-adornment, instead of disappearing into some grand design.

I was growing up. So was B. We were encountering the daily drill of life together that would someday sustain us both. But we weren't there yet. I might have longed for a home, but B. hadn't yet exorcised the demons of darkness. The hardest time was yet to come—and it would come soon.

B. started to shoplift clothes. This was in France. B. had gone back to France because, cured of pneumonia, she thought she must start life somewhere as a dancer but was afraid of the obvious place: New York. It was too big. It was too serious. She went instead to a summer *stage* in Avignon—a dance convention where many teachers taught.

It was just an excuse for more roaming.

In a green Avignon gym, among the body swings of the José Limón technique (up, down, and around), the idea came to B. that she wasn't a very good dancer. One of the teachers, a blond, wavy-haired ex-partner of José himself, told her this gently. B. hadn't had enough technique classes and couldn't ever have them. She had started too late.

But if she wasn't to be a dancer, what could she be?

She *must* be a dancer. But another teacher—small,

French, male, with a bullet head and a big nose—
yelled at her for flapping all over the place. He had the
students doing a fast clown walk with pumping arms
to a tape of Donald O'Connor singing "Make 'em
laugh, make 'em laugh." It was a tribute to American
vaudeville. This had excited B.: *her* music, *her* words,
in a sea of French. She'd thrown herself into it but he'd
said, "Stop, stop. You use too much *énergie*."

Then he said "*ridicule*" under his breath.

B., shamed and subdued, felt a familiar old bitter
emotion at the edges of her brain: purposelessness.
She was alive and the mother dead. Why?

She began to detach from the idea of being a
dancer. But not from dance itself; it was too beautiful.
Avignon yielded a final, Watteau-like performance in a
garden after a rain. On an old stone stage under big
dripping trees hung with lanterns, the teachers, little
mythical figures, leapt and chased each other in and
out of light and shadow. The figures included even the
small bullet-headed Frenchman and his dark-haired
wife in a surprisingly liquid duet.

The elusive scent of vagabond theater, of "shreds
and patches, of ballads, songs and snatches," of ordinary humans *transformed into wandering players,*
seized B.

If she couldn't do dance she might do Theater, or
rather Mime, a cousin of dance because it too was

wordless. That idea came to her at 3:00 a.m. on a sleepless night in the Avignon dorm. Paris was the center of Mime. She took the train to Paris and enrolled in the Mime school of Jacques Lecoq. Each student would work for two years to find "his inner clown." If you knew your inner clown, thought B., you would know your own kind of dance even if it was a grotesque dance. And then you would know everything.

Me, I did not like big red noses or skinny pants or floppy sleeves. I did not want to become a vagabond wardrobe flapping around and looking existentially ugly. I wanted Home, anywhere that Home could be found. I wanted to settle into a closet somewhere and work out what I'd learned about Myself through the agency of the bathrobe. I wanted to think and make choices and become mature.

And B. knew it. That is when she began to shoplift. It might have been a last paroxysm of the compulsion to wander endlessly over the earth and endlessly switch costumes, thus avoiding the inevitable tryst with sorrow. Or a compulsion to sever with Me, because I was asking for coherence.

At that time it was easy to shoplift in France because nobody did it. The stores weren't prepared, not even the department stores. From the Galleries Lafayette, B. walked off with forest green overalls of thin wool. Not loose overalls but tight Parisian flamenco-like pants that zipped up the front to below the ribs. They were a little too tight but promised to wall in the stomach. That's why they had to be stolen: they were not practical; they were not wearable; they were an idea— of suavity, of Frenchness, of Brigitte Bardot.

B. stole an idea.

The next day she went back and removed something else without paying: a pair of round-toed red, white, and blue almost–saddle shoes, with the red "saddles" on blue soles, and white laces. The shoes signaled what she thought she should be giving off: a gay insouciance.

In the tiny Paris hotel room with the old oval mirror on a stand, she put on the stolen items, the green toreador pants and the cartoon shoes, which had not been designed to go together. She looked at herself in the mirror and saw: the image she was supposed to be searching for. Herself, a clown.

It was a self she didn't recognize; it was *ridicule*. It had wide green legs and big colorful feet. It had nothing to do with Me. The B. in the mirror was joined to an entirely different wardrobe, a stolen one.

It was as if B. had struck Me a mortal blow.

All this happened a day before Mime school would have started. B., fleeing something unspeakable, went to the travel agency three stores down from the hotel and booked a flight to the only place left to go: New York.

New York. Mecca of wardrobes. City of transformations. Home of *Mademoiselle,* where B. had longed to come as a summer Cinderella.

What a pitiful state I was in when I first greeted you . . .

B. couldn't even see New York as the plane approached. Mist and rain obscured the ground. The inside of the airport seemed dark too; only the chrome pay phones glimmered—but whom could B. call?

She took out her little address book. She leafed through it; she found her beloved college tutor, now a professor at Princeton. "You're back!" said the tutor into the phone. "Please come stay—I'm in pain." The young man she'd been living with had walked out on her the day before.

So here is B., heading down Wiggins Street in

Princeton, on a night smelling of cold rain, wearing the old striped bell-bottoms, the rubbery parka, a scarf knotted at her neck, and carrying a beat-up beige suitcase of the mother's (containing the rest of Me, such that I was).

She finds the right house, number sixty-three, brown-shingled. The door swings open; a yellow light; a cry of welcome . . .

Next picture: B. at four the next morning, in a grayish nightgown, a borrowed gray sweatshirt, and borrowed thick socks (I had *nothing* to offer) alone in the tutor's yellow kitchen, surrounded by dark windows, hunched over the kitchen table with a magazine, papers, and pens spread around her. She has heated up the milk for café au lait; she holds the coffee mug and stares at the paper. On the long plane ride from France she'd asked herself: What do I do? Who can I be? Somewhere over Nova Scotia had come the answer: writer. Once she'd loved writing school papers in the evening quiet, in her room with the big trees outside. Now in the predawn kitchen she is relearning that craft.

But she hasn't told anyone yet.

Another picture: B. and the tutor, both in bell-bottoms with long, scraggly hippie hair, B.'s dark, the tutor's blond—sitting, talking, gesticulating, on the narrow white stairway to the attic. They talk for hours, about themselves and the future, about which kind of pain is worse, the predictable kind (the tutor's being abandoned) or the unpredictable (B.'s mother dying).

The latter pain has sent B. zinging around the world until a week ago. Now she has landed and is incapable of doing anything but sitting like a cat in a warm house in the company of a human. All her faculties are tuned to one frequency: the frequency of kindness. Unbeknownst to her, something bitter still churns inside her. But inside this house, for a moment, she is safe.

And I'm not needed. Which is good, because I'm not ready for New York.

And yet . . . it lies out there just beyond Princeton. Ballet classes are going on there and the life of dance that B. still longs to know about. One gets there simply by boarding a bus at the Tudor-gabled midpoint of Princeton Village. One can wear anything on a bus. So B., wearing the old parka, takes the bus. She stares out at woods, houses, rivers, vast swamps, and finally, in the distance, across a river—like mismatched teeth sticking up in some vast lower jaw—Manhattan.

She makes her way uptown. She takes a ballet class in a famous studio upstairs on upper Broadway, where the walls are Wedgwood blue and the dancers all sinew and muscle, after which she drifts downstairs and into the store next door, called Charivari (medieval term for noisemaking when an older man marries a younger woman). Here are floppy velvet hats, fabric flowers, shirts of many colors, also rows of sober gray suits and serious coats, made of the finest wool. B., in the worn rubbery parka, feels out of place. The store, a famous one—though B. didn't know it then—is run by a parchment-pale albino black woman with a cloud of light reddish hair, who smiles wryly, even at people like B. who might not buy anything.

Three times a week B. comes into the city, goes uptown, has coffee in a worn green coffee shop across the street from the ballet studio, goes to ballet class and does the best she can; then drifts into Charivari and fingers the clothes. Sometimes it's crowded, sometimes empty; B. is transfixed, as in the old days at Biba.

Finally, under the gaze of the red-haired lady, and to stop herself drifting toward nothingness, B. buys something.

When I recall this I ask Myself: how could B. have been so lucky, like a blind person hitting a bull's-eye with the first dart? She bought a wool sweater-jacket of dark green, with a shawl collar, a waist-skimming shape, and dark green buttons up the front. It was chunky and sleek, like a carnival sweater and an office sweater in one. It was one of the crossover items Charivari offered in those days, when the store was confidently navigating, almost by itself, a sea change in fashion circles. Wild and wispy sixties hippie garments were stiffening in the onslaught of the next fashion wave; they were turning into the demure yet jaunty office clothes of the Mary Tyler Moore set.

The sweater-jacket had a foot in both these worlds. And it gave Me a glimpse, the way a drowning man gets a glimpse of a life jacket, of what I wanted to become in the city: chic yet relaxed, suave yet naive. The sweater-jacket could smarten up anything, even the Appalachian dress with the pink gibberish on it.

Because of the sweater-jacket, B. got a job in the heart of high fashion. This came about one day when B. had returned to her old green coffee shop, after tramping all over the West Side with a dancer friend from Avignon, asking doormen about an apartment. Slumped in her booth, she opened her favorite column in *Mademoiselle,* "Eat," which told about its writer installing bookshelves for cookbooks in her dining room, and a rocking chair and standing lamp.

B. began to float on this vision of home. In a trance she got up, went to the pay phone, called *Mademoiselle,* and asked to speak to the "Eat" writer. The writer came on the line. "Come see me in two hours," she said.

Writers at magazines don't accept calls from the general public, much less invite the public up to see them. The "Eat" writer did. Maybe she was in an expansive mood. She could afford to be. She wasn't just any writer, she was *Mademoiselle*'s managing editor, Mary Cantwell. The switchboard operator had said so.

Paralysis gripped B. How could she just get up and proceed to *Mademoiselle*? What could she say to a managing editor? At that moment the sweater-jacket in its close-woven woolness made itself felt on her skin. Once again I was protecting her, by means of the one garment that would serve the circumstances. B. proceeded to the glass Condé Nast skyscraper on Madison Avenue that housed *Mademoiselle* along with *Vogue* and *Glamour,* the utopian destination of each summer's twenty *Mademoiselle* Guest Editors. A light-filled lobby; a sleek elevator. On the seventh floor, Mary Cantwell's office. Across an expanse of beige carpet, behind a desk—wrapped in a cranberry shawl—sat the person in question.

She was middle-aged; a doughy face with dark sad eyes. And behind her on the wall, dwarfing her, hung a huge black-and-white photo of another white face: the pointy-chin face of the writer Colette, the old Colette, with a spun cloud of white hair, staring out at B. with the sharp black eyes of a bird of prey.

"Young ladies, enter this profession at your peril!" said the black eyes.

The cranberry-shrouded Mary Cantwell came from

behind her desk, sat down with B., and conversed under the face of Colette, about books, food, about a miserable divorce and two troubled daughters. Mary Cantwell spoke in murmuring monologues that seemed to have started before B. came into the room. B. managed to project, with the help of the sweater-jacket, an eager and passionate air.

And she was invited, out of the blue, to baby-sit for the daughters. She was also invited to leave behind an essay of her own, the one she'd begun that first dark morning in the tutor's Princeton kitchen, about a suburban girl's awe at the ordinary, and sensuous, daily food of France. *Mademoiselle* would actually publish it in a few months. Best of all, at the end of the interview, B. was sent upstairs to the top floor, to the Condé Nast Employment Office, where an elegant older lady named Mrs. Hobson found her a job.

But heavens, what could she wear to work at Condé Nast?

Here began a strange time when B. served almost as a fashion arbiter herself, just when I, her wardrobe, was in My sorriest state. The job they'd given B. was not at *Mademoiselle* but at the nonliterary *Glamour,* in the Readers' Mail Department. *Glamour* was the darling of the building; it had ten times more readers than its literary sister, and they were loyal readers. They wrote to the magazine with their most intimate questions.

"Dear *Glamour,* My husband is graduating from college in four months. What do I wear to the graduation?"

B. sat all day typing the answers, recorded earlier by her boss in a soft southern voice and relayed to her through the large rubber earphones of a dictaphone.

"Dear E.J. in Michigan," B. typed, "For your husband's college graduation a creamy beige linen suit would be perfect. Look for one with a softly tailored cardigan jacket and an easy skirt (one with pleats if you like . . .)"

Afternoons the boss herself, Peggy Burlin, would enter, flinging off an aubergine cloak smelling of crisp fall air. This older Southerner with upswept gray hair made sure that every *Glamour* letter writer got a letter back, and her answers had a lilt like lullabies. She'd once run a magazine herself, during the war when the men were away. She'd "put it to bed" all through the night, once a week. She was the widow·of an avant-garde painter. She had a purple belt in Karate. She was a devotee of the New York City Ballet.

B. loved this boss. And I (in My ragged state) loved her clothes. The tight-knit wool of her coats. Her darkly exciting colors: aubergine, purple, cobalt blue. I loved even more the somehow familiar clothes of Mrs. Hobson in the Employment Office: gray tweed skirts, coral cardigans, soft navy suits, big pearls at the neck, stockings with seams. Mrs. Hobson's clothes reminded Me of the paternal grandmother, who at that moment lay dying of lung cancer in a New Hampshire hospital, refusing all visitors, including grandchildren, out of angry vanity.

Even Mrs. Hobson's scent was familiar from this grandmother: tuberose laced with Listerine. Sometimes B. went upstairs just to smell Mrs. Hobson. And Mrs. Hobson for her part seemed to like the bedraggled B. She said she had "eyes peeled" for a better job for her, a writing job.

The older Condé Nast ladies were B.'s refuge. The younger "Condé Nast girls," B.'s peers, were not. In the elevator, going up in the morning and down in the evening, these girls with their shining straight hair under whimsical hats, their plaid skirts and smart boots, their smooth leather bags in which they rooted for lipsticks, would be chatting on about photo shoots, fittings, lunches, while B. in the sweater-jacket stood silently in the corner for six long floors.

B. didn't try to talk to the Condé Nast girls, and they didn't talk to her.

But one day she made a desperate bid to belong to them. She'd left work for a doctor's appointment. On the way to the doctor she saw, in the window of a small shop on a downhill East Side street, some rose-colored velours pants, which she stopped and tried on. They had a tight pelvis and wide legs; their color was softly radiant. They were Ellen Tracy pants, way too expensive. But B. had a flash of herself wearing them to fittings, shootings, lunches. After radical calculations involving food and rent money, and grim vows to buy nothing more for months to come, she bought them.

The memory of the buying feels strange and lonely,

because it was done almost without My participation. The sweater-jacket hadn't yet restored My belief in Myself. I was a spectator to B.'s desperate lunges toward transformation.

For two weeks B. in her rose velours pants stood proudly in the elevator and made special trips to the coffee cart, though she didn't speak and wasn't spoken to.

But one day, sitting at her IBM Selectric, typing from earphones, she saw thinning patches on the thighs of the pants, where the velours was disappearing and the threads underneath were showing through. The next day the patches got bigger. It was as if My decrepit condition had taken over and decreed that anything B. touched should turn to rags. Back in the store on the downhill street, the languid salesgirl said too bad, B. must have rubbed up against some furniture.

Ellen Tracy became at that moment a malevolent person who wished her customers ill—and I have conducted, since that time, a personal boycott of her garments.

Something else went wrong at the time of the pants: B.'s face. Unsightly red blotches began to appear on it. I'm afraid I must name it: acne. B. never knew what part of her face these blotches would claim next: nose, cheekbone, chin. As the pants fell apart, the face was rebelling. Nerves, said the doctors.

I was distraught. A body without a face can't find its shape; without a shape, a wardrobe grows distraught.

Pills were taken, lotions applied to skin, "foundation" was added to the makeup routine. A pudding face looked out at B. from the mirror, with evasive eyes. In the elevator B. shaded this face. It was just then that Mrs. Hobson summoned B. to say that a writing job was opening at *Glamour*. B. resolved to show herself bravely, as if nothing were wrong. She made the proper appointments, talked to the proper people, gave them her article from *Mademoiselle* and a few small pieces she'd written for *Dance Magazine*.

"You're not quite ready for this job, dear," came the response. "Maybe in a few years."

Was it the writing? Or the face and the mangy velours pants?

Impossible to know, but Readers' Mail was now a dead end. A convivial lunch with Mrs. Burlin, a tearful goodbye to Mrs. Hobson, and B. was gone from the glass skyscraper on Madison Avenue.

On the way out she paused on the sidewalk and looked back up at the building—one inert girl among the bustling figures. Cinderella ejected from the palace of fashion.

B. had moved by then to Manhattan with two dancer roommates, to a big, cheap apartment at 108th and Broadway. She had her own room. She shut her door in the mornings and sat at her desk, reviewing notes, consulting programs, staring out the window. Then she would type furiously on a blue electric Smith Corona left over from college. She was writing reviews of avant-garde dance concerts, and miraculously, they were getting published, not in Condé Nast magazines but in little periodicals that paid in momentary exposure and very small coin.

Then she found a half-time job in the afternoons, across town, in the office of the doctor-curator of a collection of rare medical books in New York Hospital, where it didn't matter what she wore. In a basement office she wrote letters and organized conferences.

The job didn't take up a lot of time, and without the need to buy new clothes, she could save money.

So I began a period of lying low, of regrouping, of attempting to wait out B.'s listless and hostile attitude, which, strangely enough, was encouraged by something in the air, in the roommates, in the apartment itself.

When B. had fallen out of Condé Nast, she'd fallen from one city into another. This new city was called Downtown. B. and the dancer roommates (one a saucer-eyed blonde with boy-cropped hair; the other a big brunette with a classical profile) lived uptown but belonged to Downtown. They went downtown for dance classes at the studio of Merce Cunningham. He was the avant-gardist with the ballet technique; his studio, a clean clear space high among the water towers of Greenwich Village. They went to dance concerts in downtown hole-in-the-wall theaters. They sat around downtown kitchen tables lit by single candles, drinking red wine with foreign dancers also studying with "Merce."

And they wore what Downtown wore: jeans and old ponchos. B. bought an old striped Ecuadorian poncho in a used-clothing store. Downtown was stern about its clothes. They had to be lowly. No more dress-up. B. understood this suddenly in one of the downtown concerts, called *Paris/Chacon* (Chacon was a little place in

New Mexico), whose two choreographers, Ping Chong and Meredith Monk, strolled arm in arm in sweet antique clothes to some wistful accordion music, after which a chorus of younger blue jeans–clad dancers with red bandanas at their necks burst onstage singing and wielding hammers.

"Part one is an elegy, to the old anxious clothes of the Establishment," said B. eagerly to one of the candlelit kitchen gatherings. "Part two is a hymn, to the future, to honesty!"

Yet this future seemed to bring B. no joy. In the privacy of her room she tried things on, yanked them off, threw them to the floor. And there wasn't much to throw. She could never decide what to wear outside. It was worse on days when her face was bad. But her general mood was dark. The darkness inside her seemed to have enveloped her psyche, extinguishing even the usual sources of hope: the stores. B. didn't even glance at new clothes in shop windows anymore, only sometimes at old ones in junk shops.

She'd lost interest in Me, so I grew listless. I can barely remember Myself in those days: a motley mix of the old bell-bottoms and parka, the threadbare velours pants, the Ecuadorian poncho, the Appalachian dress, some hacked-off jean shorts, the sweater-jacket (but it was fraying a bit), and a long blue woolen Salvation Army cape that B. had bought on a whim in Greenwich Village, but it wasn't warm.

The problem wasn't Downtown. Other Downtowners wore their rags with élan. The problem was B., who wasn't responding or sending any signals to respond to. I couldn't hear echoes of Me inside the B. whom I had grown up with. She was like a violin left out in the rain. I couldn't play her.

Maybe it was men. The grad student was long gone. B. was sleeping with other men, though none of them twice. The roommates had habitual boyfriends who would stay for dinner in the big corner kitchen; B. just brought someone back from a party or a concert, then sent him away. Once she brought a black guy in nice sunglasses up for the afternoon. She'd met him on the street. Other guys came late at night: a distant cousin ejected from the family business (B. felt sorry for him); a just-divorced historian with an always-untucking crumpled shirt (this one had the nerve to ask B. why *she* looked disheveled); a short Armenian poet in an old-fashioned button-down shirt and sweater. This last was the one who impregnated B., but she got an abortion—mildly traumatic.

Of course it was the times, that now-infamous seventies moment of free-and-easy sex that took place like breathing, with no consequences, or so it was believed. But easy sex didn't sit well with Me. It exposed B.'s precious body—My canvas, My pristine page—to strangers. And for what? "For pleasure," B. said to the roommates, "like coffee after lunch or an after-dinner drink, those things the Midwest doesn't teach you about."

In My opinion B. had confused "pleasure" with another feature of Downtown just then emerging: the woman unbound. The second roommate, the brunette, a health nut, brought home a telephone book–sized tome called *Our Bodies, Ourselves,* by women for women. It was full of grainy snapshots of women who were not pretty but rather ordinary and lumpy. Some were in jeans and laughing; some were nude and reclining. One shot showed a nude woman sitting against pillows, holding a mirror between her legs so she could look at a part of herself she'd never seen.

"They *like* their bodies. They *know* their bodies," admonished the brunette roommate. But B. was embarrassed. "Naked" had not been a part of her and My growing up. Of course she'd had to change clothes and be without them in the transition (in her room, in the ballet studio, in the school locker room . . .). But "naked" had been a nothing state, or a "lower-class" state only glimpsed in a troubling perfection, in *Playboy* centerfolds. Now it was supposed to be a good and shameless state, especially the lumpy version of it. Bodies were supposed to welcome their nakedness no matter how imperfect, and anyway there *was* no more "imperfect."

But what was *I* supposed to do with this new "naked"? Wrap it tight? Give it room? B. didn't seem to like being naked even if she wanted to. When she slept with the men, she wrapped herself in a towel and slipped into the bed only in the dark. Maybe she'd confused being naked with having sex. But here I couldn't help her. The towel wasn't clothes, and I was always nervous.

The only time I could relax in those days was when B. sat alone at the typewriter in the oldest rags, her body forgotten, her face set in concentration.

What was the matter with her? Had something hardened inside? Was I lumped in with that something, despite the grieving and roaming we'd done together?

Nor was it just Me whom B. had shut herself off from. She never called the father. She didn't mention the dying grandmother—not even to the roommates, not even to the ex-tutor in Princeton whom she went out to visit on lonely days. Nor did she make plans to go north to the New Hampshire hospital, defy the ban on visits and see that grandmother. One of the brothers did that, and he felt better later.

B. was fighting a homesickness she wouldn't admit. But you can't fight something that's not outside you but actually there inside. You have to acknowledge it. That's what I think. And then you have to work with it, at least on the surface.

It is My opinion that bodies should strive by means of their wardrobes to keep up a brave front.

B. couldn't do it, right then. At any rate, I couldn't reach her, to help her try.

B. was invited to a party given by French *Elle* magazine (there was no American *Elle* yet), because of some translations she'd done for them. She should have worn the sweater-jacket, frayed though it was, but wore instead, to be stubborn, the torn Ecuadorian poncho, some old jeans, and scuffed brown boots from one of the roommates.

At the party she met an *Elle* writer, just arrived from Paris, wearing a peasant-style dress of crisp black cotton embroidered with blue and red flowers and belted at the waist, shiny black boots, a white headscarf tied in back, and big sunglasses.

This apparition acted like a thunderbolt on B. "Your dress is wonderful," she told the writer shyly in French. "It's not a stuck-up dress like the other people are wearing. It's a *peasant* dress and peasants are The People. But," she added in a smaller voice, "it's not dingy or drab like . . . my clothes."

The writer herself, Jacqueline, had a French murmuring-sighing kind of voice and an attentive face with a strong jaw and delicate, chiseled features.

B. invited Jacqueline to a downtown dance concert; then they went to dinner at a bistro with Christmas lights strung on the ceiling. They ate plates of spaghetti and drank two glasses each of red wine. B. explained that dance was "the pulse of the city"; that dance "taught the writer to make the words move." Jacqueline listened so avidly that B. also decided to mention the car accident that had killed the mother. Jacqueline in turn told B. about what she called her too-perfect life in Paris, which was why she'd fled there for "*la Bohème de New York.*"

Strangely enough, Jacqueline seemed to admire B.'s unkempt clothes. "*Elle se fiche de son apparence!*—she doesn't give a damn how she looks!" wrote Jacqueline excitedly that night in her journal. That's what she later told B.

B. and Jacqueline continued to meet, and became friends. But I got the most from this bond, since B. was exposed, at every meeting, to someone on excellent terms with her wardrobe.

In My gradual New York rebirth, which I'm describing here, Jacqueline had cast herself as fairy god-mother. A few items from her trunk even found their way to B.'s closet. She said she didn't wear them any-more, but I think she just wanted to give them to B. The best was an orange-and-black dress of chiffon (lit-tle black flowers on an orange background), by St. Laurent—*St. Laurent!*—which, she said, "went better with your dark hair than with my fair hair." It had a bodice gathered at the waist and sleeves gathered at the wrists, like a peasant dress. But it was gossamer.

B. hung it in her nearly empty closet, in the middle of the rack, and fingered it reverently almost every day, though she couldn't figure out where to wear it, or with what shoes.

When the paternal grandmother died, I mourned her and My earliest mentor, her wardrobe. But B. was occupied with other things. A minor miracle had brought her a contract to write a book about the beginnings of modern dance. She'd met, at a party, the queen of dance critics, a dark-haired and snappy older writer, who'd sent her to a book editor, who'd in turn given B. a book contract.

Real writers lived alone, so B. decided to move. She went on a search and found two oddly shaped rooms farther downtown, on a ground floor, giving onto a beaux arts courtyard. She told herself she didn't have time to think about the grandmother's death. Too much to do.

And if the roommates were dismayed because the house would break up, too bad.

In the midst of B.'s move, four brown-paper packages arrived in the mail from New Hampshire, addressed to B. in the paternal grandfather's small rounded hand. Inside the first, on top of some velvet items, lay a letter in the same hand. "Here are some clothes that belonged to your grandmother's grandmother," it said. "Her name was Susanna Beaumont." In a postscript at the bottom of the page, he'd written, "Your grandmother wanted you to have them."

The velvet items were three jackets in jewel tones with whalebones in the bodices. One was garnet red, one emerald green, one darker maroon. The garnet one had points dropping below the hips, Harlequin style. B. had never heard of this French great-great-grandmother, who'd lived in Davenport, Iowa.

The second package contained a long black silk skirt folded lozenge-like. The third had a high-necked faded white blouse with big sleeves, and another long black skirt, with small white half-circles printed on the silk and a big ruffle around the bottom. The fourth package, smaller, held an old doll in an antique white lace dress, with a bisque-porcelain face and amber glass eyes with an almost-human light in them.

B. sat on her bed, in bell-bottoms, holding the doll, surrounded by the silks and velvets. I was thrilled. This was My heritage, the several-generations-back heritage most wardrobes never get to see. But B. was sad.

The jackets didn't fit her. What should she do with them? It seemed this unknown great-great grandmother had been a small woman . . . But one of the skirts was bigger, the one with the half-moons. It almost fit.

On her last night in the apartment, B. put on the half-moon skirt and a sweater that covered its safety-pinned waist. Downtown dancer friends came uptown to drink red wine. B. walked around in this voluminous lush black silk skirt with the serious, hem-level ruffle. Everyone was impressed with it. It swished as B. walked. The ruffle was weighted; its heft made B. straighten her back.

How grand it must have been, long ago, to be a woman in Davenport, Iowa. That's what I was thinking.

After the party B. put the half-moon skirt in one of the cartons earmarked for the new apartment, along with the almost-human doll. The velvet jackets and the other skirt she wrapped back up in brown paper and stuck on a high shelf in the hall closet. The movers arrived, hoisted the moving cartons, took them twenty blocks downtown to B.'s strange new apartment with the glass doors onto the courtyard.

The other clothes in the brown paper just stayed in the old apartment, with the roommates. B. forgot about them, or maybe she remembered them but didn't do anything about it. The blond, saucer-eyed roommate called many times to remind her to pick up the packages from the hall closet. "Yes I'll come for them," B. said.

But she never did.

The roommate called one last time. "I took the clothes to a fashion museum and donated them," she said.

"You did what?" B. shouted into the phone. But she ended the conversation on a polite note, since it was her own fault that the clothes had gone unclaimed.

Those disappeared clothes are still a sore point between B. and Me. How could she have abandoned things worn by her own great-grandmother? How could she have thrown away My heritage?

She wasn't yet ready for a heritage, or even for a past. She was gambling on a future, and that took energy.

But you cannot reject precious things and be okay.

I'm a mood barometer, I know.

Ambition had entered the picture. You have to be Somebody to write a book, so B. started acting like that. Where she'd been silent and unresponsive, now she sent Me a flurry of signals. But they were crazy signals. I couldn't make out what she wanted.

Still, I attempted to rise, Phoenix-like, from the ashes. One day B. went, as if sleepwalking, to the hair salon of the Mod English hairdresser Vidal Sassoon (in the ugly white General Motors building on Fifth Avenue) and got her bedraggled hair clipped to a geometric mop, with small points descending in front of the ears. Of course the old Downtown Me didn't match the new hair, so B. rushed to Charivari and bought a blue jersey halter dress with black chevron stripes. A sleek cap of hair; a torso of stripes—a symphony of geometry.

The money for the transformation came from a foundation grant for the book. The inspiration came from the bizarrely named Twyla Tharp, the cutely deadpan choreographer who had kidnapped downtown dance and brought it uptown. Tharp herself had been a creature of limp hair and worn jeans, but she had gone earlier to Sassoon and acquired the first (in the dance world) upside-down bowl of hair. Then she'd started to toss her head around onstage, so the bowl of hair flew around; then she'd adopted old jazz and witty costumes like backless tuxedos, injected twitchy ballet into the mix, and tried her best to show that the avant-garde and the mainstream were one and the same.

B. tried to do this too, or made Me try. But it didn't work. The cute and trendy straitjacket I'd been forced to put B. in made her spirit curl up (and Mine!). She found this out when she went, in her geometric dress, to the mountaintop wedding of one of the younger brothers, in Maine. The other guests, wearing old jeans and droopy tunics from India, wouldn't meet B.'s eye. And she couldn't meet theirs.

This charade ended at a midwestern university, where B. was flown out to give a talk on the subject of Twyla Tharp—looking, alas, just like subject. She stood at the podium, in the geometric dress, shaking her Sassoon mop, and speaking in tart and manic fashion.

It was ridiculous, and B. knew it.

So she abandoned geometry and adopted sophistication, of a sort. This came about because of the New York City Ballet, and the queen of dance critics. From the stage of the cool gray-stone State Theater at Lincoln Center, heavenly dancing by Balanchine and heavenly music chosen by him washed over the audience. In intermissions in the airy lobby, critics formed groups around the critic queen, B.'s dark-haired distant-mannered friend with the crisp pleated skirts and two-toned shoes.

Everyone in the groups vied to be witty. B. hovered for a long time on the edges of the groups but gradually slipped inside, and made some remarks. The queen of critics invited B. for coffee, then to dinner, then, on another day, to a shopping stint in Saks Fifth Avenue. Amid the sale racks, the critic took a Geoffrey Beene suit from one of those racks and handed it to B.

"This would look nice on you, dear," she said.

The suit had a gathered skirt of beige-and-green

tweed, a dark green satin blouse with a string tie at the neck, a short, fitted, unlined jacket of beige wool. And the name of its maker was sacrosanct. He was an intellectual designer who made old-fashioned hour-glass shapes with new-fashioned means (he hated linings).

B. bought the suit for a tidy sum, even on sale.

A dream come true, a Designer Suit, by a semirogue designer. And yet, away from the store and the queen critic, the suit didn't settle right. Its gathered skirt enlarged B.'s hips; its satin tie at the neck enhanced a wide-eyed air B. knew she could summon but was tired of. That dutiful blouse-tie seemed like a throw-back to the smug time of the raw-silk dress—and I can't stand smug.

After a few outings that suit was retired to the back of B.'s closet, where it stayed, wreathed in the sad aura of money misspent.

Then B. fell under the sway of a Russian immigrant bal-let teacher with an earthy aura. This teacher had appeared one day in a studio in Carnegie Hall, teaching a ballet class that wasn't detached and neutral like the ones B. knew, but picturesque in a Greek and Oriental way. The teacher was thick-necked, black-haired, gold-toothed. She danced like a portly Scheherazade. She danced, to B.'s eyes, not like a ballet dancer, but like one of the early-modern dancers in B.'s book. She had just emigrated from Russia and was heartbroken about that.

B. went to visit her one day, wearing a jeans skirt with overalls bib, at her apartment in the immigrant neighborhood of Sunnyside, Queens. The black-haired teacher met B. at the door, looked her up and down, and said, "You have no right *clothes*." Another shopping trip resulted, this time to a new store B. hadn't heard of but that the just-arrived Russian teacher had, Loehmann's. It sold cut-rate designer clothes.

The teacher moved through the racks and handed B. a black knit tube like an elongated sweater, with a cowl neck, that tied at the waist with a knit belt.

"This good for buy," she said.

B. expected the dress to give her the earthy, sexy aura of the ballet teacher herself. But when she wore it to the theater, it constricted her walking to small steps. In the knot of critics gathered around the queen critic, B. grew tongue-tied.

As I'd shown B. before, countless times: tight clothes cut off access to free thought.

That dress went to the back of the closet too.

Here I was, a collage of other people's wardrobes, a bunch of extravagant and useless items that hung uneasily in the closet, unable to fraternize with one another, or combine in an identity. As for B.—one day she was geometric with zigzags; the next day, hourglass classical; the day after that, sexy and earthy, and some days she reverted to the happy-go-lucky look of overall skirts. Her hair went long or short, loose or pinned up, straight or permed (she got several smelly "permanents"), according to the demands of the outfits.

B. was all different people—that is, she was nobody. And I was nobody too. Except in the mornings, in the library, when B. sifted through boxes of old reviews, photos, dance programs, letters, making notes on index cards. That's when she could forget about Me, and leave Me and My (at that moment) old anonymous self in peace.

A famous English dance impresario came on a visit. He had a long face and beautiful pinstriped suits. He was introduced to all the young critics, but it was B. he asked out to dinner (she wore the tight black

Loehmann's tube) and then to his hotel, even though he had a wife in England.

Why? Maybe he liked B.'s showing off, and My awkwardness. His own clothes were very fine, especially the fabrics, from the light wool of the suit to the cotton of the shirts and the jersey of the boxers. I derived some comfort from those clothes—which is probably why B. thought she'd fallen in love.

B. flew to London to visit this guy while his wife was away. But in another woman's bedroom, in another woman's kitchen with her cooking stains on the butcher-block table, in her living room with her dainty yellow armchair, B. grew silent and numb.

After a dance concert, sitting with the impresario in a lamp-lit London restaurant, she asked if he was tormented by his own duplicity.

"Why should I be?" he answered.

On the day of the wife's return, B. and the beautifully suited man left the apartment together in the morning, he with a briefcase, she with her luggage. At the end of his little street, he said, "Ta ta," and went off toward the Underground. B. wasn't due to leave for another two days. She paused, then carried her suitcase to a call box. She dialed a woman she'd met only once, a dance photographer. "You can come here," said the woman.

When B. arrived with her suitcase the woman gave

her tea, made her a bed on the couch, and lent her a bathrobe so she needn't unpack. The bathrobe was a long cotton kimono-thing sporting a blue design of ancient Japanese teahouses. It took the shape of B.'s body as she sipped her tea and told her story. It curled around her in the night as she slept her troubled sleep.

Toward morning B. woke in the dark not knowing where she was, smelling the borrowed bathrobe. She'd been immobilized once before on a stranger's couch, in a borrowed bathrobe. Had we come round again in a circle, no closer than before to a style of our own?

In predawn London, despair hits many.

But unbeknownst to B., we were headed for a breakthrough.

The breakthrough had something to do with taking *off* clothes and starting again at zero, with just the body.

Back home again, B. decided to learn the dances of Isadora Duncan. It was for her book; it was research. A group of older ladies, forgotten by most of the dance world, met every week on the upper floor of an old two-story gray building in Midtown. They'd been students of the six adopted daughters of Isadora.

When B. climbed the building's stairs, to the dressing room, the ladies' matronly suits lay neatly folded on benches. In the studio beyond, they themselves, in featherweight crinkled silk tunics laced under the breasts, threw their heads back and reached high with their arms. Aging angels against the light of the window.

They became B.'s teachers, and she received, from their fund of Duncaniana, her own featherweight sleeveless tunic of yellow silk, which was crisscross-laced under her breasts and around her ribs, and slit up the front of each thigh to permit vigorous locomotion.

Wearing the yellow tunic, B. let her knees bend, her pelvis float, her shoulders hang in the manner of a body newly released from corseting, circa 1905. The body that was B. traveled back in time. She reclined on the ground with a handful of other young women, lifting up an arm in salute to the sky; she stood up and took the asymmetrical pose of a Tanagra figurine; she gently shifted position to become another figurine.

She learned whole dances, leaping and skipping heavily to Schubert piano tunes, joining hands and whirling with the other dancers.

And I too traveled back in time. As the crinkled silk tunic (the garb of Renaissance angels), I clung better, shimmered better, moved about on B.'s body better than I had in a long time.

A transformation was wrought. At home in the bedroom B. stopped throwing pieces of Me on the floor. She stopped wincing at her mirror image; she even smiled at it sometimes, before venturing out. Duncan dancing caused a long-delayed blooming in B.; it was as if a fountain of sensation, dammed up by a years-long spasm of grief and anxiety, had started to flow. With this inner release, B.'s body dropped into itself. Her breath filled her lungs; her hips received her torso's weight; her legs smoothed themselves downward; her calves felt their power; and the bones of her feet made happy little clicking adjustments to support the suddenly, physically radiant (with the absence of self-loathing) B.-in-motion—not just in dance class, but in the streets of New York.

This small explosion of corporeal well-being affected even B.'s work. At her writing desk, the finished pages piled up.

Isadora became at that moment our patron saint. It seemed as if she had given her blessing to B.'s particular body with its womanly hips and thighs, its too-thin calves and ankles. As if B. had borrowed from Isadora not just a surface style, but an inner classical roundedness, reinterpreted by a wild California body.

"The highest intelligence in the freest body" had been Isadora's wish for the American woman. We wardrobes are the secret ingredients in that recipe.

B.'s new vibrancy of skin was conveyed to Me with her every move.

I could almost say I was happy, for the first time in My adult life.

Just then the Museum of Modern Art was honoring the film pioneer D. W. Griffith and showing even his earliest movies, the Biograph Shorts. On the screen appeared, as if risen from the dead, a Lower East Side New York street scene of 1912, complete with live people, crowds jostling and gesticulating—and in their midst, filling the screen in close-up, the earliest movie stars: Mary Pickford, with her long corkscrew curls; Lillian Gish, with her dreamy eyes and little mouth; both wearing fitted wool dresses buttoned up the front, skinny jackets nipped at the waist, plaid shawls, big round hats with feathers, little lace-up boots.

These dresses weren't stiff the way B. had thought old-fashioned clothes were supposed to be; they were supple. They moved with their wearers. Not only that, they were loved. You could see this from the way Pickford and Gish smoothed their skirts, gathered their shawls, held their heads high.

The clothes offered what those girls, and maybe the actresses themselves, needed to survive in the big city: a little dignity, a little style. Clothes were a serious business in the city of those movies. One whole Short, *The New York Hat,* treated Mary Pickford's longing for a flowered hat in a store window.

And B. herself, at the other end of the corridor of time, longed for one of those old-fashioned dresses: in particular for the checked suit with long skirt and trim jacket worn by Mary Pickford in a longer movie, *Amarilly of Clothes-line Alley.*

She vaguely looked about in old-clothes stores but couldn't find anything like that suit.

However, Jacqueline came from Paris just then and brought B. something from a new boutique called Agnes B. It was a jacket, a trim one of stone-colored linen, with three stone-colored buttons. It had an old-fashioned, nipped-at-the-waist look about it, but it was smooth and simple too.

A jacket! As much as B. had wanted the *Amarilly* suit, she hadn't thought one could be found, much less a piece of one. Jackets had been so absent from the scene, in the flower-child/lumberjack years, that this one seemed new and futuristic, even as it was old-fashioned.

In fact, Agnes B, a real down-to-earth person in Paris, was making a new kind of plain clothes, humble like school uniforms, yet *urban,* meant for the new version of the city woman. And beautifully cut, in the French manner. Unobtrusively well-cut. The linen jacket could go over anything and lend its wearer a touch of that poor-girl dignity displayed by the Griffith heroines, now rendered timeless in the linen jacket.

Wearing it, B. waded into conversations, animatedly talking, not standing mournfully aside. The linen jacket shows up in the memory of B. conversing with a book agent at a party, a tall, svelte, redhead. B. needed an agent. "Okay, let's talk," said the agent, and B. felt at that moment a click of delight, at being shown off to the agent by the mock-old-fashioned linen jacket.

Of course you could say it was B.'s finishing her book that gave her this sudden animation. She'd done something. She'd made something. She'd even moved out of her ground-floor fishbowl apartment into a third-floor walk-up, tucked in the back of a brownstone, with a balcony over green gardens.

But I too had played My part in the birth of the new urbanized B. And not a small part. With wardrobes and bodies, it goes two ways. The body chooses the clothes (or in the jacket's case, Jacqueline had chosen *for* B.). But the clothes on the body allow it to absorb whatever aura the clothes were chosen for.

What was it about a *jacket*—a garment born on English country estates, passed on to women via horseriding and cycling—that invigorated B.? Its newness and its oldness. Its jacket history. The linen jacket brought the sportiness, readiness, ease, and urbanity that matched B.'s inner wishes at that moment, that matched the role she was ready to play in her new life. It marked a step up in B.'s readiness to engage with the world.

My autobiography is coming to an end, since at this point I'm on the verge of becoming Myself. B. is almost thirty. The linen jacket was the first piece of the new Me in which I felt all the necessary elements present. What are those elements? Simplicity, authority, relaxation, *fit,* and a nod to the theatricality that accrues to life in the city.

A silver cuff bracelet was the second revelatory piece of the new Me. B. had seen several silver cuffs, made by Navajos, on the wrists of the head of production of her book publisher, with whom she'd had conferences about how her book should look. This production head was a woman, at home in a man's world. B. went with the production head to a printing plant, to watch her own book covers spewing from a huge machine: thousands of sepia covers, each with a white-tunicked Isadora dancer on it.

The next day B. made a quick trip downtown to the production head's favorite Indian store and found, this time, not an imitation cuff but her own cuff (no two of these Navajo cuffs are alike). It was stamped with thunderbirds and lightning bolts.

The jacket, the bracelet: here began a proper balance, for Me, of old world and new, of sleek and defiant—of all the things that felt right for now and for the time ahead.

The book was to be celebrated at a party at the agent's house. But what to wear?

B. had searched in vain for a book party dress in all the right kind of stores, including Charivari, but everything looked fussy. One day, though, she found something in an old-clothes store (they weren't yet called vintage stores). It was a piece of cream chiffon bunched up in a bin. B. unbunched it. It was a really old dress. It had elbow-length sleeves, an oval neckline marked by tiny delicate vertical pleats, a self-tying chiffon belt at hip level. It was embossed with squiggly satin circles enclosing etched crosses. It vaguely matched the Duncan dancer's white tunic on the book cover.

"Yep, it's twenties," said the fat proprietor of the old-clothes store.

The twenties, when women had morphed into tubes—

tubes in motion, tubes gyrating, with propellor-like arms and legs, or with long swinging strings of pearls; when the crustacean paddings of femininity that went back over the whole previous century fell away to reveal the woman's body as a sleek androgynous living torso. B. had conjured up the twenties in her book. Now a piece of that era had floated into her possession—a talisman of the bodies that had discovered the twentieth century.

At the agent's apartment, a setting sun spilled through big windows and lit up blush peonies in vases and a lot of people milling, laughing, talking, gesticulating, eating raw vegetables and flaked-off parts of a large pink cooked salmon. Among them floated the dark-haired B. in her cream-colored drop-waisted dress. At this time, a decorated chiffon dress looked odd and unexpected. *Because* it was old. No other wardrobe, then, that I knew of, would have allowed its body to wear *someone else's* old dress to a party.

I had been a prescient wardrobe. In hindsight the dress appears to mark a divide, between the time when clothes were supposed to be always new (or to look so) and the time of vintage, when Fashion began to cannibalize its own past.

But even wearing an antique dress, B. didn't stand out that much from the other guests, since all of them had made an effort to look singular and celebratory. It was, after all, the end of the seventies. Those guests, like B., had lived through the decade-long slow-motion clothes upheaval. They had wardrobe doppelgängers of their own, with whom they'd struggled, with whom they'd learned to collaborate in the performance of themselves.

The red-haired agent-hostess wore a Sonia Rykiel sweater and skirt of white knit wool that clung to her tall, sinuous form. Others in the room wore everything from a multicolored ethnic vest, to a red-print African dress, a white peasant shirt, a bright blue double-breasted suit, a pair of yellow sandals, a black lace vintage dress over a black underslip, a crocheted coral dress over a gray underslip, white harem pants tucked into black boots. There was a smattering of bodies in tweedy sweaters and a small but critical mass (certain feminist scholars) wearing sober gray and black.

It is bittersweet now to imagine those ghostly party-goers. So many have died, taking their smart radical exuberance with them, like multiple suns being extinguished. None believed at that moment they would ever need wear again or do again what had been prescribed for them in their Main Street youths, in the ranch houses, tenements, mansions of their hometowns. They thought they had found perfect freedom and found it easily. How innocent they were. They didn't know that ahead lay AIDS and death, or old age or failure or unbearable regret. B. herself was at that moment sleeping with three of the party guests, none of whom knew about the others. But all the party guests, including B., were headed for pain and unbearable regret.

This party marked the end of many things and the beginning of others. After it, B. would take her first steps toward the then unknown (to her) mode of loving just one person, of trying to find a balance with just one person, not with all the people she had slept with in that permissive time.

But that's another story.

Yet this story also ends in monogamy—the monogamy B. was finding with Me. We were settling down. We were making some kind of commitment right then, to stick with each other and grow together. We would be rejoined from this moment on in a kind of free-flowing wisdom, as we'd been joined at the very beginning, in childhood, but without the wisdom. Here at the party, even with the confusion of multiple lovers, the unit of B. and Me was making a faint lunge toward happiness.

Suddenly, in the midst of this fragile happiness—in the triumph of the antique chiffon dress in the setting sun—a lonely thought came to Me.

B.'s twenties dress had once belonged to some other

body—now lost, if not dead. Pieces of a wardrobe might last longer than their bodies, the way souls are supposed to last longer.

Pieces of Me might live on when B. was gone.

Would I even still be Myself?

B. awarded herself a small trip to Europe, to celebrate the book, to reclaim that time when she'd been so lost, before she'd come to New York and found a profession. She went first to Nice, to see dancer friends who lived on a hill with an orange tree. From Nice she took the night train to Venice, to visit the Renaissance paintings Isadora had loved—the real ones, not the reproductions—which hung in churches and palazzos.

At 5:00 a.m. the train made a stop in Milan. B. and a Swedish guy in the lower bunk stumbled out to the station to find some coffee. Afterward the Swedish guy trudged off in the dark to a student hostel, and B. went back to the train.

But in her compartment there were no people. Also no suitcases. The luggage rack was empty.

B.'s suitcase was gone, with most of Me in it.

"Oh my God," B. cried. She ran to the door of the car. Dawn was just lighting up the tracks. "*Sono rubata!*—I've been robbed!" she yelled from the open door, dredging up the phrase from *La Fanciulla del West,* her favorite Puccini opera.

And I—I was panicked. Did I still exist? Had I died? What could I be without My *matériel*?

B. rushed back to the station to get help before the train left. Two Italian policemen sat in their already hot office on the edge of the tracks, chuckling. "Looks like the gypsies went through the train," they said. "You can stay here or go, but we can't do much."

"But everything was in that suitcase!" B. cried. Yes, everything: the zigzag dress from the Sassoon days, the green sweater-jacket from Condé Nast, the Appalachian dress with the pink gibberish, even the black mourning dress (now too short) from the mother's funeral . . .

B. ran back to the train and jumped on as it started to move. Three hours later she rode into Venice's sleek white Mussolini-era station with nothing but the clothes on her back and a pocketbook. A lone figure, with pocketbook. Bereft of belongings, drastically lightweight, a human balloon about to rise up . . . she walked into the city.

By evening she'd calmed herself enough to sit in a

lamplit restaurant near her *pensione,* composing a letter to the Nice friends about the interesting state of luggageless-ness.

"It's like being released into perpetual vagabondage," she wrote almost happily. And I too had calmed down. After all, I'm not the inventory of the clothes, nor even the specific items. I'm a spirit. I'm the sum, at any given moment, of a lifetime of impulses about how one body needs to look— impulses that turn into experience, then pass into knowledge. And there was something more. I had reached, all unplanned, without fanfare, a kind of personal apogee. The outfit B. had put on when she left Nice, the outfit she still wore in the lamplit restaurant, was as trim, sleek, jaunty, free-moving—perfect—as I'd ever managed.

It consisted of dark tan canvas pants from Willi-Wear, a scoop-neck vest of woven salmon nylon, the stone-colored Agnes B linen jacket, the silver cuff on her wrist, rope-soled black espadrilles on her feet.

It was a suit (with accessories)!—that masculine fixture turned icon of modernity. Although, with top and bottom in two beige shades, the suit had a *slant rhyme.*

The WilliWear tan pants, bought back in New York, were the key (pants always are). They closed by means of a tying arrangement emanating from a crisscross waist panel, like a sash, secured with a little brass buckle with multiple holes. That's how they could take the exact shape of B.'s waist and hips. These pants had been invented by a tall, shy black man named Willi Smith who would die of AIDS seven years after this moment, but not before he'd dreamed up the new category of American homespun-elegant.

The clingy salmon vest had come from a booth of cheap clothes in the street market of Ventimiglie, Italy, right over the border from Nice. The vest had three fake-silver buttons up the front. It was one of those magic items that arrive by chance, as in a fairy tale. It fit nicely over B.'s bony chest and shoulders. It was good under the linen jacket. Its buttons matched the silver cuff bracelet.

The black espadrilles of rope and canvas on B.'s feet had come from the street market too. They were fishermen's shoes, sold by the bundle, so they'd cost almost nothing.

But it truly doesn't matter to Me if the pieces are cheap or expensive. The task of a wardrobe is to try to encode, or reveal, in tongue-in-cheek fashion, the oscillating impulses that have made a body itself just at that moment, using whatever garments are at hand. And I'd done that. I'd made a sartorial portrait of the inner B., as she sat in that cozy Venetian restaurant writing a letter. The jacket said "urban"; the silver cuff said "tough"; the pants said "sinuous/practical"; the vest and espadrilles said "tan skin" and "summer."

The whole outfit said something else as well, something bigger. After all, this book is not only the story of one wardrobe's struggle with its body, but of a generation of wardrobes: where We came from; where We got to; how We did it.

I'm taking here the long historical perspective. Let's say that wardrobes of the West found modernity first in the figure of the flaneur dandy, that singular nineteenth-century Paris city observer, strolling through the streets in suave black suit and snowy white shirt and cravat, sporting a cane and maybe a turtle on a leash, empathizing with all, detached from all. *Free to be anyone,* because of his anonymous clothes, yet always himself, the man of leisure, the man of means. He haunted the nineteenth century.

So who's not to say that here, in the late-twentieth-century traveling outfit I'd assembled for B., was a light, unfussy, beige-toned *female* version of the flaneur's costume? A costume mixing high-class elements and low, restraint of line and extravagance of fabric. Who could deny that here was the *flaneuse,* absent from history till now (except for stray *lionnes* like George Sand in flaneur days)? The woman with the privilege to roam, and to register her roaming on her very skin; the woman as modern vagabond, wearing an outfit embodying freedom for its wearer—the freedom to sleep in a train, have coffee in a station at five in the morning, walk into Venice with a light load and a light heart.

Women had almost never before been allowed to explore cities as solo figures, undisguised, except maybe in the radical 1920s (and then not in pants). Their clothes—and behavioral conventions—had kept them from this. B.'s present traveling clothes were as momentous as those dandy clothes of the earlier century. What they marked was the first time in Western history when women could be out on the streets; could be of the city yet detached from it; could be seen yet not seen—invisibly visible. Could be *left alone*.

The day after the suitcase theft, B. woke early in her little *pensione* with its back window looking out on a narrow canal. She'd slept in the nude; the nightclothes were gone. She put the *flaneuse* outfit back on. She counted her traveler's checks: four fifties, so one for Me. Instead of heading for churches and palazzos, B.

went back to the train station neighborhood, to a Standa dimestore she'd seen on arriving. She made her way through the shouting Italian moms and kids (the inside of the Standa was just like the street) to the clothes, where I was put to the final test. What did she need? She already knew, or rather *I* knew, because I'd become Myself. Here's what she bought (swiftly, unhesitatingly): a long denim skirt, a coarse-woven, white peasant blouse, a lavender cotton nightgown, a red nylon shoulder bag with braided handles to hold it all.

These Standa clothes would fulfill their promise. They would take B. through a week of roaming among the churches and palazzos of Venice. They would mix well with the *flaneuse* pieces—and I would be, for a while, a pocket version of My newfound self: an easy wardrobe, not flashy but handsome; a wardrobe that favored good ideas but didn't call undue attention to itself.

I was settled, but in flux as well, like all good wardrobes.

And here is where we leave the story of B. and Me—at the moment when B. came out of the Standa, clutching the red nylon bag that held the new (yet not new) Me. She stopped, surveyed the raucous street scene, then set off back into the heart of the old island-city of faded splendor, into a series of narrow streets and little bridges, toward a succession of ancient stone palazzos with peaked Oriental windows leaning over pea green canals. She stared at façades. She went in and out of churches with smoky interiors and dim altar lights. She visited palazzos that were museums. She went up their wide or narrow stairs. She peered at their ceilings, floors, furniture, paintings. She looked out of their windows, at the dark, ever-so-slightly-moving water of canals.

In the last palazzo of faded mint green, up its grand worn stone steps, on the second floor, in an oval baroque hall, B. raised her face to a painted ceiling and stared upward for a long time.

Then she smiled. The ceiling showed blue sky, white clouds, golden light, and a bunch of naked cupids gazing down at her.

They, of course, were in heaven, so needed no wardrobes at all.

If this book were a movie it would end here, with a slow pullout from that baroque ceiling. You would see the rosy flesh of the cupids in their gold-blue sky, then, as the camera moved back, the entranced B. in the tan pants and linen jacket, staring up at them, clutching the red nylon bag; the crowds of tourists milling about her in the long oval room . . . You would pass through the palazzo wall to see the green walls and Moorish columns of its façade; farther back you would see more palazzos—and then the whole island cityscape of domes, steeples, and minarets, surrounded by the gleaming Adriatic . . .

And you would get the impression I intend you to get, that B. had moved definitively into the world, clothed, but with the freedom of nakedness and the cloak of anonymity. In that short week in Venice she would encounter all the nooks and crannies of the city as well as the churning waters of the sea on its every edge, with the sky opening out at the ends of streets.

And when she went home to the place that finally *was* home, New York—another cityscape of stone and sea—she had become unexpectedly lighthearted. So had I. It was as if the bitterness that had been inside her for so long had dissolved in that ceiling of blue and gold. She talked about what she'd seen, with the friends who were now her urban family. She wrote about Venice in her journal, as she would, in the future, talk, think, and write about a host of other things.

And I, as B.'s many-colored and protean second skin, would come along in that future, to do My job of presenting her, protecting her, eliciting from her a continual stream of sharp, intimate sensations about the state of being alive.

Don't forget: We wardrobes exist, in the end, so that Our bodies can forget Us, so that they can plunge into the world, showing themselves as they wish to be seen, taking in (unimpeded by shame or discomfort) whatever of the world's offerings come their way.

Fade to black.

EPILOGUE

Fade up to gray, twenty-five years later.

A rainy day. Gostini Dvor in the rain, the ancient, yellow-stucco shopping arcade on the main Nevsky Prospekt of St. Petersburg, Russia. It's a neoclassical, two-story rectangle interspersed with fat white Colosseum-like arches. Inside on the perimeters: endless white corridors, lined with shopping areas and clogged with damp shoppers—and one of the shoppers is B., striding down an upper corridor, wearing a shimmery dark green belted jacket with a black fur collar and wrists and a black fur cap with one earflap down.

What is B. doing here?

She lives in New York. But she's got a grant to be in Russia this fall and winter to research her latest book (while I do mine). B.'s still a traveler. And she's long felt the pull of Russia: Tolstoy, Turgenev, Leskov, blinis, Fabergé eggs, famine, war, siege, heroism, suffering, torment; the curlicue excess of Tsarist times; the plebeian palette of later times; and through it all, the Russian ballet.

B. still loves and writes about dance.

Usually she's in an archive all day, sifting, in the light of a Soviet plastic lamp, through old telegrams, petitions, diaries, reconstructing a lost and perilous world. But on the way to and from the archives she passes through the modern city, if it can be called modern. Pastel palaces with iron filigree balconies line the streets and the canals that wind through the streets. The river Neva, as wide as the sea, splits the city down the middle, so the view from one bank to the other looks like, as Joseph Brodsky wrote, "the mollusk of civilization."

But even with a head in the past, B. is a body in the present. A foreign body not-from-here, who must be carefully dressed to blend in with the inhabitants, on the streets, in buses, on metros. She's a chameleon by instinct; she likes to match the environment. So I must be especially observant.

Russian women dress up for the streets. Many are beautiful. Older women wear chic scarves draped over coats, and chic fur berets or fur cloches that do not look like the hats of hunters and trappers. And womanly boots with heels, sold in the many shoe stores of this snowy, rainy city. Under the coats are usually skirts and dresses, not pants. Some younger women wear jeans but they're designer jeans, also paired with heels and smart coats. There are no light blue dumpy jeans in the picture, or track shoes. No dumpy parkas. No unisex safari people padding around, other than the occasional American tourist.

And no women masquerading as newsboys, waifs, addicts, or ragamuffins.

Style here seems a throwback to the days when women in cities dressed up, just because a city is a theater. But in one costume only: *femme.*

Russian women did *femme* even before Gorbachev raised the iron curtain, and even if they had only one nice outfit. B. was here then and saw these single nice outfits worn day after day. How did women find the clothes then, with no shops, no neon, no ads? In elaborate secret ways.

Those were smart wardrobes.

Nowadays the Western chains have moved into St. Petersburg. A Mango, a Levi's, a Colins (British jeans), a Mexx flaunt their tough stuff up and down Nevsky. But Russian wardrobes, even young ones, haven't succumbed. *They* get replenished from hole-in-the-wall shops in new urban malls, where some chic girl sells the single items she's carried back herself from Milan. The Russian wardrobes have held on to their dignity.

It's as if a corner of urbanity has survived here intact—as if Paris in the fifties had jumped forward to the Russia of now.

This is interesting, at least to B. She wants to explore this Russian femininity. I think she wants Me to incorporate some of it into Myself, like skirts and pointy-toed boots, even if I'm dubious.

But how do we find it?

Just after she got here, B. began to notice certain white plastic bags everywhere in the city, carried by all different kinds of Russian women. The bags said "Oggi" in plain gray letters on the white (our letters, not Russian ones). "Oggi" means "today" in Italian. It must be a store, B. thought. An Italian store? She made a vague resolve to find out. That was a few weeks ago. Then yesterday, in one of her archives, she forgot a plastic bag for pen and notebook, so the house-wifely (uniformed) police guard in the corridor fished in her own purse for one to lend, and out came—an Oggi bag.

Even the police guard! That's why B. is striding, this Sunday afternoon, toward a portico in the middle of one of Gostini Dvor's corridors, embellished with a white neon OGGI sign. It might hold the secret of feminine aplomb; it might produce a new B., at least for a moment. There's always that hope.

She passes under the portico. Oggi has a sovereign

space in the corridor, filled with L-shaped racks of clothes. Rows of clothes also hang along the walls. They're in two-color groupings, like in the West: a pink and brown section by the left wall; a plum and gray section on the right. In front of B., indigo and black jeans and tops.

B. moves the jeans to see one pair—sprays of amber jewels fan out on one leg. She reaches up to a pile of beige sweaters on the next rack—they're shot through with gold threads. She proceeds to an all-black section of corduroy jackets and skirt—embroidery! Big red and turquoise flowers march up these jackets' fronts. They are beautiful. Unfortunately B. is *wearing* a black corduroy jacket bought last winter at H&M. But the skirts have embroidery too: arrows, chevrons, little houses sewn in turquoise and rust.

Everything is so decorated it's almost funny. Even I am charmed. But this is not the glitz of Rodeo Drive. The Oggi glitz has a whimsical Russian twist, as if arising from an ancient cultural impulse to embellish. Think of peasant scarves and woodcarvings. B. checks with a salesgirl about Oggi's origins. It's from here, Petersburg, a *Piterskaya Firma*. The Italian's just for show.

Or else it's in the cut. The jeans are tight. The skirts are tight then drippy. The blouses are nipped at the waist, like the top half of the hourglass. B. picks out a magenta shirt of thin corduroy that sends out a pure enjoyment of womanly shape. I say okay, maybe. It's like a cartoon that thinks it's real life. Oligarchs' wives might wear such shirts, dining with nervous husbands, as beefy tracksuits stand guard. B. takes another shirt, a blush pink crinkled cotton one, from the brown and pink by the wall. Same vampy cut; nice color. She heads for the dressing room.

Then she doubles back to the black corduroy rack and grabs up one of the embroidered skirts.

"Wait a minute, B.," I say. "I'm not exactly a flirty-skirt wardrobe."

"Give it a chance," B. tells Me. "Open yourself up to the surroundings. Isn't that your job?"

Yes it's My job. And I'm going to do it, even if I'm not sure I want to at this moment.

B. pulls the curtain closed in the tall dressing cubicle. She takes off the rakish fur hat, shakes her hair free (it's short and newly dark reddish), hangs the fur-lined coat on a hook, takes off the black corduroy jacket and gray T under it, strips off the black ankle boots and the black velours pants . . .

And stands in front of the mirror, in black camisole, pink thong with a broad band of lace at the hips, and black socks (the socks that always look stupid in dressing rooms). She observes herself. The stomach creeps over the lacy thong. The upper arms jiggle if she taps them. The inner thighs are melting. The knees—B.'s knobby knees that used to embody her cocky self—they've gone mildly reptilian, as if the flesh were puddling to small wrinkles above them.

And the face . . . it's tightened. B. has acquired the hawklike look of the father and the fierceness of his dark eyes. And the skin around the eyes is yellowish, like parchment. True, Oggi's lighting is particularly ghastly. But the tired circles under B.'s eyes are visible, even if they're supposed to be neutralized by the yellow paste in the Lauren Hutton makeup box (it usually works).

The irony is that B.'s *figure,* as an outline in space, has never been better. It's long and lean from all the walking she's done in this city; it's molded nicely to the skeleton. It still carries the hint of a pear, but even that feminine swell at the hip and butt looks better these days, even to B. herself. Also she holds herself without hunching, unless she forgets, and then I remind her for God's sake to *stand up straight.*

But B.'s stuck at the moment on the *unhappy flesh.*

She looks away from the mirror. She pulls on the embroidered corduroy skirt. She zips it up. It's gored down the hips. It fits perfectly. She looks back at the mirror.

"Well?" she says.

I'm about to say yes. The skirt's whimsical, like a maiden's in a fairy tale. And I have a weakness for magic signs on cloth.

But B. is stepping out of it. "I can't do it," she whispers. "I'm too old."

This event complicates things for our femininity expedition. B.'s reaction to the mysterious aura of age has been, up till now, a deep astonishment. How did age settle on her? And when? Inside B.'s torso lives a column of energized air. On the street she never walks, she strides. She lunges up stairs. She runs for buses. Her mind is fired up with questions about history. She is not old.

But just now she's had one of those dressing-room jolts that occur when an image in the mirror collides with one's impulse to look fresh and vital. The jolt brings a small seismographic interruption in our usual harmony. B. seems to feel some foolishness in front of Me, exacerbated by the flimsiness of the Oggi space in the giant old shopping arcade, where everyone is more or less of a younger generation, in a city where B. knows people but doesn't really know them (yet) and doesn't have the friends of home to complain to—and anyway, it's a harsh life here, walking miles in the rain and cold between subway stops.

B. used to get these jolts all the time when we were young. Back then she would be alienated for weeks, as in our London days, when she lost her bearings in the underground palace of Biba. Now equilibrium returns almost at once. Here she is, outside of Gostini Dvor on the rainy sidewalk, clad again in the shimmery jacket, opening a small red umbrella, heading into the crowded underground passage under Sadovaya, her black back-pack clutched against her right side (the pickpockets here love backpacks), a white Oggi bag clasped in her right hand. It contains the blush pink shirt, which fit nicely, even if it's oversanguine about a *bosom*. The magenta one was too big.

What's happened to B. in the quarter-century be-tween then and now?

First, of course, she got old. But that's not all bad. "Old" for B.-aged people doesn't mean the deflation of before. B.'s not going to suddenly acquire a lot of limp Chanel-ish suits and move to the back of family pho-tos. She's going to experiment—*we're* going to experi-ment—and be seen. Because I'm old too, as old as B. I'm a senior wardrobe by now. But I'm not conflicted about it. A lot of experience resides in Me, so nothing is forbidden. Just some things don't feel right, like the embroidered skirt I almost succumbed to.

Second, B.'s life has momentum.

She's emerging from the tunnel now, passing, on the right, the edge of the huge gray library with white cornices, which stretches down the side of its own Ostrovsky Square (two thousand employees—one of the great libraries of the world). She'll go there tomorrow to read Tsarist documents.

It's a strange life. She's always researching a book and writing it. Like being in school forever. She teaches in a college too, though not this semester. She never married. She doesn't have children. She is someone who's doing now what she always did, which is the only thing she ever wanted to do.

Now she's on a level with Ostrovsky Square, where bare trees wait for snow and the bronze of Catherine the Great looms on its round base, wreathed by a circle of her (smaller-scaled) lovers. B. hasn't lacked for love. She's had grand romances of the "Wild nights wild nights / were I with thee!" variety, shot with longing, despair, flashes of delirium and hard-learned patience. A few of them lasted years, like marriages. One's in place now, though it's tapered into friendship, anchoring B.'s heart, freeing much energy. Some were secret. Some were with men, some with women.

B. has reached the Fontanka Canal. She crosses the bridge with the four rearing bronze horses and the near-naked bronze men restraining them; she looks down the curve of the canal toward the ever-diminishing pastel palaces. Past it she turns right into her own side street, then into a brick courtyard with lamps over doorways. She ascends in the clanking elevator, deploys the several surgical instruments on her high wooden door, puts her backpack down onto the table with the huge mirror, takes the white Oggi bag into the bedroom with its eighteenth-century blue-glass chandelier, opens the door of the ancient wood *garderobe* (it means "wardrobe" in English) . . .

And *voilà.* Here I am.

Or rather, here is a small selection of Me, chosen for B.'s Russia time.

But at this point I'm going to take movie-camera license and fade the old Russian *garderobe* with its few traveling items, into the big closet at home surrounded by bookshelves, where resides the rest of Me—the whole of Me up to this point. I want to do an inventory. I want to take stock, to remind B. about the particular and timely femininity that's come to be her own, but that seems to have slipped her mind under present circumstances.

Open *those* cream-colored closet doors back home

and you'll find, in the temporarily deserted closet, a lot of clothes, maybe more than women of modest means used to possess. On the left hang pants in dark colors and a few black skirts. On the right hang shirts in color blocks—beige, then white, then black, then a few greens blues oranges—and, below them, a crowded row of little jackets.

But it's not just Me that's overpopulated. Every wardrobe I know has swelled up. Clothes in the world have multiplied. This went on under the radar of Fashion. (My definition of Fashion: a provocative, perverse, exclusive, sexual force that swoops down from above and drops occasionally brilliant outrageous ideas on Me.) This clothes-multiplication had something to do with the Fishers, Don and Dorothy, the San Francisco couple who couldn't find the right jeans in 1969 so started their own store to fill in the gap between the generations, a store that has cloned itself on a prodigious scale.

Now wardrobes don't have to strategize to acquire precious pieces for their bodies' dowries. They acquire and discard, acquire and discard, at an ever-accelerating pace.

I'm not implying that I've turned into a Gap wardrobe. I have not. What you could say instead is that the world caught up with Me. Today, everybody who buys something in a Gap or a Gap spawn can be seen as a *flaneur/flaneuse*. Any woman, anytime, can get hold of the pieces that make up that once predominantly masculine body envelope: two legs (trousers), two arms (shirts/jackets). My lifelong struggle to get away from the just-feminine (the struggle that's momentarily slipped B.'s mind)—that's over. There *is* no more feminine, in St. Petersburg terms, except in St. Petersburg (and Moscow). There *is* no more age.

Just thousands of street-smart pieces of clothing circulating in a never-ending cycle.

Sometimes I worry about the poor clothes waiting to be bought. So many of them, twisted and strewn about in megastores. Separated from their piles. Agitated by sound waves. They can't *all* find bodies to take them home. What happens to the ones left over? Do khaki-white-denim bales of them lie moldering on docks next to bunches of bananas?

But I'm not a wardrobe that marches in lockstep, whatever the intentions of the clothes multipliers. Take the white shirts in the closet. White shirts are a staple of Gap and of all the clothing stores that resemble it above and below on the store hierarchy, but My white shirts are one-of-a-kind shirts, each acquired for a different reason. Some weren't even bought at all, but passed moneyless to B. from friends, as loans or gifts. They speak, as they hang there, about the web of human relations that has formed around B. since she and I came of age. And about the moments of B.'s existence that have piled up into a life.

Here is a translucent, barely ruffled rayon blouse, bought by B. in her home city from J. Jill, because she'd been invited to give the graduation speech at her old girls' school, and wanted something delicate. Here's a square-necked thick-lacy peasant blouse with cloth buttons down the back that looks old-fashioned and dowry-like—S. brought that back for B. from Bucharest, Rumania. A long tuxedo shirt with pleated front—passed on from the wardrobe of M.'s (B.'s best friend) deceased thin-framed African American father, an elegant dresser—which looks good with pearls. A Russian designer tunic (pre-Oggi vintage) of cream-colored linen with little Constructivist red wheels around the heart, bought in St. Petersburg in an earlier summer, when B. taught at a writers seminar. A crisp, snap-closing, cotton-nylon white safari shirt with a secret zip pocket on the shirttail, ordered through the mail from the Ex Officio travel catalogue.

In their origins the shirts are a mixture of male and female. But they've been transformed by B.'s wearing them. Even empty and unworn while she's away, they still give off memory-scents of B.'s living moments.

The translucent ruffled one has the spirit of that garden party after B.'s graduation speech, when people were impressed and the late-spring sky was a soft blue. The Russian tunic retains the nervousness of her reading her own work at the writers' seminar, and the funny-serious belief of poet friend Brenda that red around the heart helps readings. The Ex Officio shirt smells like the sudden cheer of a lonely moment in Finland, when its half-synthetic crispness restored B.'s spirits.

And each of the seventeen others has its own account of where it came from and what it lived through with B. If you could chart them all on the grid of B.'s life you would get a thousand flashes of B.—so many points of white-shirtness that they eclipse the question of masculine or feminine. You would get a symphony of white-shirted B.s, and surging up in that symphony, if the composer were good enough, would be something of My own archaic-poetic history that crosses gender lines.

These shirts are emanations after all of the ancient unisex idea that white belongs next to skin, manifested in the linen under-tunics worn by the very clean Egyptians, the snowy white shirts of Parisian dandies, the belted tunics of Russian peasants, the starched high-neck shirtwaists of Gibson girls, the flappers' unisex middy blouses, the white robes of Negro baptisms . . .

The shirts even *smell* like whiteness—lavender-ish, flax-ish—and they have that age-old smooth whiteness feel between the fingers.

The same is true for the other hanging blocs, the pants and skirts and jackets. Each piece of each bloc brings along its own intimations of wardrobe history. And each piece, besides, has traveled for a while next to B.'s skin; has caught, more than once, the scent and spirit of her.

Shirts, jackets, pants, skirts—and something else too. On the far left of the closet, almost hidden in the dark, you get a glimpse of shimmery turquoise, a flash of red, a hint of gold. These are the magic pieces.

What do I mean by this fanciful word?

One day when B. was still a young writer, she was crossing an avenue in Greenwich Village in a thin coat in a cold wind. She stopped on the other side. A cubbyhole shop she'd never seen before displayed a chalk scrawl on the window: "Clothes made from parachutes." A coat hung in that window, made indeed of iridescent aubergine parachute material lined with shaggy black fake fur, with a tag saying half-price.

B. tried on the coat. It was splendid—and warm.

She was the only customer. A thin blond boy minding the store wasn't even looking at her.

Should she buy it? At this point B. sometimes made some money from writing features in fashion magazines, but her income wasn't predictable. She hadn't published a book. That is, she was nobody. She wasn't even teaching yet. She led quite a precarious existence. How could she claim this shimmery coat that demanded bravura from its wearer?

On the other hand, the coat, still wrapped around B., was starting to tell a story that could be heard only faintly, as if from far away. Once upon a time, in a rugged old forest in France, a girl, lost in the woods, came to a rusted gate, which opened onto an avenue of gnarled trees leading to an ancient turreted castle, and inside the castle, set in a paneled vaulted hallway, was a forgotten closet in which hung . . .

Way inside Me too something began to stir, some awakening to dreams, to fabric, to glimmer, to enchantment. That something was connected to the ancient kinship I have with books, stories, ancient tales.

In short, B. bought the coat and took it home in a large brown bag. That night she couldn't sleep because the coat pulsated in her closet like a secret, like Christmas.

The next cold and windy day she wore the coat to meet a feminist historian friend. The friend was horrified. "How could you?" she sputtered to B. "It's seductive!" Women were not supposed to wear seductive garments because that meant they were pandering to the patriarchy.

That's when I absorbed the coat and all it meant into My spiritual self. The historian was wrong. The parachute coat wasn't only seductive, it was also something older and purer. Something connected with *Masquerade* and *Carnaval* and humans partaking of the power of the fairies who'd lived in the ancient forests of Europe and transformed lost girls and youngest sons into resplendent beings.

I resolved at that moment to insist on the possibility of semifantastical garb as a discreet part of B.'s daily life, no matter what some feminists say (even if I could see their point). And as My salute to beauty, or to something even more subliminal and ancient: the place where cloth intersects with imagination.

Remember the three mythical sisters, Clotho, Lachesis, Atropo, who spin, measure, and cut the cloth of every person's life? They're part of every wardrobe's aura, even if most of My fellow wardrobes have forgotten them.

There's nothing, after all, that says myths can't exist in the present as well as the past. With every garment containing a little magic, even just some glitter, I'm wrapping B. in a myth, about the ancient and transformative properties of cloth.

Do you see, B.? This is My femininity, and yours, and it's older than that of the ladies with the hourglass blouses, and probably deeper too, in the power of its meaning. Who's to say? But it works *in our case.*

The coat itself's long gone—its parachute material started to flake off years ago, its fake yak fur got matted. But other things have taken its place. The glint of turquoise in the closet: that's a lounging robe of silk-velvet B. found in an antiques barn in New Hampshire. It's from the twenties, like the long-ago book-party dress (which is still here as well, on a shelf in a plastic bag). B. hasn't yet worn the lounging robe to a party, since parties nowadays are hard to find. But it's there, telling her about the possibility of one.

The gold is a gold trench coat, bought one sunny autumn day in Washington, D.C., when a bunch of dance critics went down to see the then still partially hidden (behind the iron curtain) Kirov Ballet . . .

And so on. Each of the magic items has a story to tell, drawn from the world's fund of stories, or from a fragment or hint of a story.

Sometimes merely the feel of the cloth can make a

garment magic, or the light going through it, or a kind of warmth it can offer, or one row of beads that brings shine to its workaday shape. The magic clothes can even look plain on the outside; they're magic when they give B. the sensation of being swathed and protected, transformed, *lit up.*

But if those sensations are to make their appearance, B. must cooperate too.

This is our bargain: B. offers Me a torso that's been "motioned"—animated by some means, even exercises on the floor, though jogging is best, or dancing, or walking, if there's no time for anything else. I can't say this enough. A body has to *use* the muscles and skin and bones that were created in the beginning to be moved, if it wants to talk to its wardrobe.

In return, I offer B.—well, everything else. I am magic and the possibility of transformation.

I am her weather in cities where people don't get enough exposure to the sky and the stars. Instead they have wardrobes to make the weather. I can do storm clouds or sun—or their equivalents. On a gray day I can be bright. On a bright day I can be sober. At night I can glitter.

I'm a travel album, closet-size. I keep cloth souvenirs of where B. has been, what she has observed about the human raiment of different peoples and different countries.

I'm a record of friendship. So many pieces of Me were passed to B. from her friends, and other pieces of Me have gone to their closets.

I'm B.'s protector from the elements, the soother of her agitation. Sometimes, if she's exhausted and limp, I can even rekindle in her a desire to be alive.

I'm a shelter for B.'s eccentricities, because some parts of the Fashion game she cannot go along with. So I refuse too. I don't do bags, even if they are a mania these days—bags with buckles, toggles, and other hardware; bags pictured sharp-focus in magazines next to soft-focus models. B. just carries, on every occasion, one soft backpack of black leather, made by a prideful craftsman in his Greenwich Village apartment and sold on the corner of Greene and Prince streets in SoHo.

And I'm a source of sensations in her skin, of ever-shifting sensations. This may be My most important function now, since in B.'s experience, sensations are becoming more insistent. B.'s sensations, in fact, seem to be bringing us slowly full circle, or beyond full circle, back even to the pre-memory of sensations. Babies, when taken from the womb, are wrapped in receiving blankets of soft cotton. They like that, said B.'s gynecologist when queried.

Lately B. has grown very fond of the feel of clean cotton. Actually the feel of any soft fabric can instill desire in her nowadays to acquire the garment in question, even if the garment isn't exactly the right shape. I've even held her back from buying something ill-shaped that feels good—she who was once so particular about the cut! The sensation of lightness, the sensation of warmth, the sensation of smoothness: these are potent.

I think it's all part of getting older, and of B.'s skin becoming more acute in the process. She feels more keenly her own warmth under blankets in winter, and within that warmth, she feels the texture of the sleep garment she's wearing. I never worried before about what B. slept in. It used to be just any old T-shirt. Now a fine cotton nightdress is something B. looks forward to. The sleep clothes once stuffed onto a shelf in the bathroom closet—B. has smoothed them out and put them in neat piles.

"We have to grow old to conquer youth," wrote Bachelard, quoting Michelet, "to free it from its fetters and live according to its original impulse."

Sensations from Me are likely to be more in demand in the future.

On My interior map of the world, a string of stores is lit up, the way the stops on the Paris Métro used to light up on a huge wall map when a passenger pressed where she wanted to go. Here are some of them:

Marimekko, FINLAND

Although it was started in the 1950s (see My Chapter 22), this Finnish clothes company is alive and well today. Its founder-diva Armi Ratia died in 1979. Marimekko almost died too, but was bought and rescued in the early nineties by another diva-businesswoman, Kirsti Paakkanen, black-haired, who wears only black with stiletto heels, and is tall even without the stilettos. The new Marimekko makes smart new clothes, and also recycles its earlier tropical-Scandinavian cottons into hip new garments, like jeans jackets.

What I like is Marimekko's constant conversation between its past and its present.

In late May 2007 on the way to Russia, in the Helsinki airport Marimekko store, B. bought a cream-colored anorak that zips up to a funnel neck, is good for rain or wind, and looks excellent over black.

Liberty House, NEW YORK

B. found this store in the seventies, maybe because it was near Charivari. But Charivari (see Chapter 37) was always a little grand for B., whereas Liberty House was like home, because it had well-made flower-child clothes B. could afford. I regret to say that B. and I abandoned Liberty House in the eighties, when no one except utopian types wanted gypsy/flower clothes, but rediscovered it in the nineties when such clothes seemed again like a good idea. Now we check the new Liberty House (on 112th and Broadway) often; some Liberty House tunics hang in the closet next to the white shirts, some sweater-jackets (brand Sarah Arizona) lie in the sweater drawer.

Patagonia, USA

I believe that the clothes of the future will come from sports houses like Patagonia, L.L.Bean, Puma, and others (including the brands in *Runner's World*), because these houses are doing research into lightness, durability, and anatomical molding. For instance, B. will not wear bras because they dig into her ribs, but wears instead shelf-bra matte nylon camisoles from Patagonia. She owns these in white (with aqua straps), black, avocado with aqua, pink with brown— in the underwear drawer—and, in the jogging drawer, periwinkle with navy. They do not dig into her ribs, and I commend this outerwear company on its feminine engineering.

B. also has a Patagonia featherweight avocado green anorak that resides in her backpack and gets pulled out when it starts to rain, and a shiny avocado and pea green, almost weightless, down-filled pullover that offers instant warmth and stained-glass color.

LainaJane, NEW YORK, TWO LOCATIONS

Either one of these stores is My favorite for lingerie. I love lingerie, and haven't talked enough about it here. Maybe I'll write another book. LainaJane is filled from floor to ceiling with lingerie pieces that bodies can move in; that aren't just for show or titillation. The three Chinese-American sisters who run the stores (the oldest founded and named it for herself) know exactly how their garments behave. It was one of the sisters who first pointed B. toward the easy-fitting Hanky Panky lace thong, now worn by everyone at all times. Another sister recently made B. try on, for the fit, a ruched lime green camisole with a black bra-area crisscrossed with magenta lace. I made B. buy it. Rarely does one find "carnival" and "practical" in one garment.

I contain, at home, and B. used to wear, when young, a filmy, pink silk shorts-pinafore-underthing from the twenties, once called a "step-in." It's horizontal across the chest, held up by wide silk straps, adorned with rows of white lace, like a trapezoid of froth. A frolicsome body must have worn it, once upon a time, before B.

Ah, lingerie—the outer lining of a body, the inner lining of a wardrobe. B.'s and My most intimate meeting place.

Harry's Florsheim Shoes/Tip Top Shoes,
NEW YORK/UPPER WEST SIDE

B.'s feet show the effects of years of dance classes—that is, they're wide in the ball, and the left foot pronates. And they've inexplicably jumped, in recent years, from size 7½ to size 9½ or even 10 (for boots). I think I allowed B. in her youth to wear too-tight shoes. But despite pronatings and bunions, I will not permit her now to wear square and clunky shoes. The only possible solutions to the foot-comfort problem come from these two stores, eleven blocks apart. Both carry vaguely sensible yet thoughtful American-made shoes, but their trump cards are the shoes from France (the tony Arche) and Germany (the practical-minded Ara, et cetera), mostly suaver than American shoes.

Because of B.'s veteran feet, I strongly favor strengthening the U.S. dollar, since its woeful leakage from war debt means that American women's feet can be clothed stylishly only at great expense.

Norma Kamali, NEW YORK

Although this Midtown Manhattan designer store (56th Street) seems to have turned into a multi-level juice bar–cavern, I am honor bound to mention Kamali, because she was and is a great clothes visionary. I got almost drunk with admiration back in the eighties, when tailored garments made of gray sweatshirt stuff emerged from her workshop. B. once owned a jacket with built-in shoulder pads, its eighties cutthroat look softened wittily by its sweatshirt fabric.

And just the other day, B. saw, in the Kamali window, a breathtaking display of mannequins wearing sweatshirt pieces paired with gold-lamé pieces.

H&M, EVERYWHERE

No wardrobe can resist the Swedish H&M, and its Spanish cousins Zara and Mango, because whoever is designing the stuff has a mind that's in tune with, or ahead of, whatever Fashion says at the moment about proportion. However, B.'s Finnish friend U. says that wardrobes must be wary of these mass-produced trendy garments, because they were made by little Cambodian fingers.

It's hard to keep that in mind.

I found the Karl Lagerfeld black-and-white H&M collection of 2004 a thrilling event. B. has a pleated black chiffon skirt with *chiffon-covered buttons* from this, H&M's first venture into high fashion. The subsequent Madonna collection was a dog.

Gap, EVERYWHERE, BUT ESPECIALLY THE UNITED STATES

Obviously I have mixed feelings about Gap. Its garments err on the side of bland, like many U.S. mass puveyors. Why are these brands so afraid of *ideas*? The timidity of Gap sometimes, Ann Taylor *always,* and Talbot's—yuck—makes Me crazy.

But recently Gap/Red (not the color but the line-within-the-house, like a publishing house imprint) has rescued the mammoth chain for B. and Me. Red-label clothes are said to benefit AIDS-infected Africans, and display safari-rustic trappings vaguely evocative of hippie days and great adventures.

I believe in checking Gap/Red every once in a while. A faded red-leather Red belt with brass ring buckle keeps low jeans in place on B.'s hips.

Olive & Bette, NEW YORK

The first of the soft form-fitting T-shirts showed up fifteen years ago in Liberty House, from a company called Grass Roots. Liberty House still has good Ts, but in My opinion the best Ts nowadays come from this little Manhattan chain. Designers named Splendid and James Perse seem to be finding ever-new tucks and scoops that show bodies off, and ever-softer cotton to make the shirts from.

B.'s small, lithe, olive-eyed, quietly suave niece Alex arrived in Russia last fall carrying only a red backpack, whose contents sufficed for ten days because of an array of T-shirt pieces that worked for every occasion, even for the birthday of a proper-minded balletomane.

Note to My fellow wardrobes: T-shirts are recommended only if your body-protégée is in shape.

Oggi, RUSSIA

On a recent trip to the newer Oggi store on Petersburg's Nevsky Prospekt, B. found a denim pantsuit with Baroque black braid trim. The jacket hugs the ribs like a corset (with hooks instead of buttons), gathers itself at the shoulders, and ends at the bottom in a discreet black ruffle. The narrow jeans themselves have black lace trim around the waist, mostly hidden under the jacket's black ruffle. Its message: I am a jeans woman with a long-submerged, suddenly unearthed heritage of palaces, carriages, courtiers.

Only Russia, with its wild inquiries into its own identity, could produce this futuristic Baroque stuff. Also its fashion designers have, up to now, received rigorous, classical educations.

The Potato Barn Antiques Center,
LANCASTER, NEW HAMPSHIRE

This long, homey white barn contains the best vintage clothes B. has ever seen (and that says a lot), plus splendid antique *things* of all kinds. It is worth traveling to the North White Mountains to visit it, since Mark and Kellyann Yelle know exactly what they are doing and appear to cherish the relics that drift into their purview.

The clothes hang tidily, protected by plastic, in their own spacious room, each with a little white tag, which notes, in Kellyann's delicate handwriting, its era—and the eras go way back to before the turn of the other century.

Such respect for old clothes brings Me to tears.

There are drawers of scarves and gloves too.

The gruff-looking Mark and the delicate redhead Kellyann make a movingly human pair. Their child, Bryce, is an articulate young man of seven.

G-Star Raw, EUROPE VIA NEW YORK

This pan-European clothes company has chosen to put its biggest store in Lower Manhattan, maybe because its combat-flavored, multi-pocket clothes telegraph the mysterious urban jungle high style that New York exemplifies. At this moment, now that B. is back in New York, G-Star Raw comes as close as possible to doing My work for Me; its clothes define the aura I would like B. to emit in most workaday settings like classrooms.

Some G-Star black cargo shorts in B.'s possession have two big side pockets and two small back pockets sporting brass buttons, but also contain a hint of belling-out like eighteenth-century gentlemen's knee-length breeches. These disparate types of masculinity combine, in My opinion, to form a tough and edgy femininity.

To B.: this is *your own* femininity, which registers the note of defiance that has seeped into the style of many Americans these days, men and women. Why do peace-loving Americans "on the left," such as B., wear paramilitary-type clothes, and the bellicose ones "on the right" wear pastels?

Everyone nowadays seems to want to fight everyone else, but some reveal it in their clothes, and some not.

With B. back home from Russia, such dire thoughts occupy Me nowadays.

I do reserve My affection for garments that manage to

signal several things at once. How can Americans today avoid signaling several things at once via their clothes, such as: involuntary arrogance (yes, even from B.), shame, obliviousness, defiance, come-hitherness, go-awayness?

My younger colleagues have a lot of work cut out for them.

Tales of Hoffmann/Grand Hotel,
ONCE-UPON-A-TIME NEW YORK

These two linked stores with Joseph Cornell–flavored names once graced West Broadway just below Houston, back in the days when brick-and-iron SoHo was miraculously reclaiming itself from slum status. I'm including them here now, so their memory won't die.

One dark and rainy night in the seventies, the young B. was struck dumb when she happened upon the lit windows of the two stores. Displayed behind the glass were three striped dresses that seemed to have surfaced from a Hoffmannesque tale. Beyond the dresses, visible on the stores' interior walls, hung several blown-up photos of 1930s Negro debutantes, in elegant white ball gowns, holding white flowers. City of a thousand stories!

B. could never afford anything from the stores, but friends' wardrobes still contain the following items (how I envy those wardrobes): a wheat-colored light wool skirt with white snaps down each thigh; a skirt seemingly made from a blue Mexican serape; a curvy, deep-wine–colored silk blouse; a pair of round-toed, step-heeled, red-velvet shoes embossed with fleurs-de-lis.

However easy or edgy are B.'s current everyday clothes, I still must remind the world, from time to time, that she is a lady. In this tricky undertaking, the memory of Tales of Hoffmann/Grand Hotel acts as a beacon in the night.

ACKNOWLEDGMENTS

The Wardrobe wishes to thank the following people, who have contributed to the writing of this book inspiration, sustenance, support, sometimes even clothes.

Family: Ibby Carothers, Mardi Kendall, Jessica Kendall, Jenny Kendall, Jaimee Kendall, Sara Kendall, Barbara Krevlin, Jane Mendelson, and the two family members to whom this book is dedicated, sister-in-law Joan Krevlin and niece Alexandra Kendall.

B.'s Students: all of them, especially Lizza, Shahira, Claire, and Gautam.

The Staff and Fellows (2004–2005) of the Dorothy and Lewis B. Cullman Center for Scholars and Writers, the New York Public Library, where B. and I worked side by side—especially Jean Strouse, Pamela Leo, Linda Gordon, Stephen Kotkin, and Colum McCann.

Friends and Mentors: Heidi Almi, Lari Angervo, Thomas Bender, Jacqueline Buglisi, Charlotte Carter, Christine Dakin, Jacqueline Demornex, Ann Douglas, Wendy Gimbel, Laurie Goldstein, Linda Gordon, Neil Gordon, Maxine Groffsky, Emilia Hallberg, Robert Haas, Outi Heiskanen, Ronnie Heyman, Brenda Hillman, Laura Jacobs, Irja Kantanen, Riitta Koljonen, Irina Kolpakova, Gabriela Komleva, Manana Kvachadze, Tamrico Kvachadze, Keti Machavariani, Irmeli Mäkelä, Claire Mallardi, Ellen Mandel, Dorla McIntosh, Kirsti Paakkanen of Marimekko Oy, Peggy Price, Phyllis Raphael, Tatiana Semenova, Leslie Sharpe, Jamie R. Wolf, Hilma Wolitzer, Leslie Woodward . . . and, for special sustained support, Stathis Eust, Ulrika Hallberg, Margo Jefferson.

Huge and grateful thanks to this book's agent, Lane Zachary; its editor, Deborah Garrison; and its editorial assistant, Caroline Zancan—for their willing suspension of disbelief and their imaginative and generous participation.

BIBLIOGRAPHY

Agins, Teri. *The End of Fashion: How Marketing Changed the Clothing Business Forever.* New York: Quill, 2000.

Arias, Philippe. *Centuries of Childhood: A Social History of Family Life.* New York: Vintage Books, 1962.

Baudelaire, Charles. *The Painter of Modern Life and Other Essays.* New York: Phaidon Press, 1995.

Beckerman, Ilene. *Love, Loss and What I Wore.* Chapel Hill, North Carolina: Algonquin Books of Chapel Hill, 1995.

Benjamin, Walter. *The Writer of Modern Life: Essays on Charles Baudelaire.* Cambridge, Massachusetts.: Harvard University Press, 2006.

Bordo, Susan. *Unbearable Weight: Feminism, Western Culture, and the Body.* Berkeley, California: University of California Press, 1995.

Brattig, Patricia (Ed.). *Femme Fashion 1780–2004.* Stuttgart, Germany: Arnoldsche Art Publishers, 2003.

Brewer, Christopher. *Fashion.* Oxford and New York: Oxford University Press, 2003.

Brooke, Iris. *English Children's Costume 1775–1920.* Mineola, New York: Dover Publications, 2003.

Brumberg, Joan Jacobs. *Fasting Girls: The History of Anorexia Nervosa.* New York: Penguin Books, 1989.

Demornex, Jacqueline. *Madeleine Vionnet.* Paris: Editions du Regard, 1991.

———. *Christobal Balanciaga.* Paris: Editions du Regard, 1988.

———. *Lancôme.* Paris: Editions du Regard, 1985.

Devlin, Polly. *Vogue Book of Fashion Photography, 1919–1979.* New York: Condé Nast Publications, 1979.

Fillin-Yeh, Susan (Ed.). *Dandies: Fashion and Finesse in Art and Culture.* New York: New York University Press, 2001.

Formanek-Brunell, Miriam. *Made to Play House: Dolls and the Commercialization of American Girlhood, 1830–1930.* Baltimore and London: Johns Hopkins University Press, 1998.

Foster, Patricia (Ed.). *Minding the Body: Women Writers on Body and Soul.* New York: Anchor Books, 1995.

Fraser, Kennedy. *The Fashionable Mind: Reflections on Fashion, 1970–1982.* Boston: David R. Godine, 1985.

Hodgson Burnett, Frances. *A Little Princess.* New York: Penguin Books, 1990.

Hollander, Anne. *Seeing Through Clothes.* New York: The Viking Press, 1978.

————. *Sex and Suits: The Evolution of Modern Dress.* New York: Kodansha America, 1995.

Laver, James. *Costume and Fashion, A Concise History.* New York: Thames and Hudson, 1969.

————. *Taste and Fashion.* London: George C. Harrap and Company, 1937.

MacDonell Smith, Nancy. *The Classic Ten: The True Story of the Little Black Dress and Nine Other Fashion Favorites.* New York: Penguin Books, 2003.

Mariana. *Miss Flora McFlimsey's Christmas Eve.* New York: Lothrop, Lee & Shepard Books, 1949.

Melnikoff, Ellen. *What We Wore: An Offbeat Social History of Women's Clothing, 1950 to 1980.* New York: Quill, 1984.

Pacquet, Dominique. *Miroir, mon beau miroir: Une histoire de la beauté.* Paris: Gallimard, 1997.

Postman, Neil. *The Disappearance of Childhood.* New York: Vintage Books, 1994.

Steele, Valerie. *Fifty Years of Fashion: New Look to Now.* New Haven and London: Yale University Press, 1997.

Tomerlin Lee, Sarah. *American Fashion.* New York: The Fashion Institute of Technology, 1975.

A NOTE ABOUT THE AUTHOR

Elizabeth Kendall is the author of the books *Where She Danced: The Birth of American Art-Dance*, *The Runaway Bride: Hollywood Romantic Comedies of the 1930s*, and *American Daughter*, a memoir. Her work has been published in a number of periodicals, including *The New Yorker* and *The New York Times*, and she has worked on several television documentaries for public television. In 2004–2005 she was a fellow at the Cullman Center of the New York Public Library, and in 2006 she received a · Fulbright research grant for St. Petersburg, Russia. She is presently at work on a nonfiction book, *Lidochka*, about the tragic fate of George Balanchine's ballerina-classmate, Lidiia Ivanova.

A NOTE ON THE TYPE

This book was set in Fairfield, a typeface designed by the
distinguished American artist and engraver Rudolph
Ruzicka (1883–1978). In its structure Fairfield displays the
sober and sane qualities of the master craftsman whose
talents were dedicated to clarity. Ruzicka was born in
Bohemia and came to America in 1894. He designed
and illustrated many books, and was the creator of
a considerable list of individual prints in a
variety of techniques.

COMPOSED BY
North Market Street Graphics, Lancaster, Pennsylvania

PRINTED AND BOUND BY
RRD Crawfordsville, Crawfordsville, Indiana

DESIGNED BY
Iris Weinstein